D1174071

creative film-making

KIRK SMALLMAN

creative film-making

The Macmillan Company

Collier-Macmillan Ltd., London

Library of Congress Catalog Card Number:
69–18815
First Printing
The Macmillan Company
Collier-Macmillan Canada Ltd.,
Toronto, Ontario
Printed in the United States of America

Many thanks to all the people
who appear in the illustrations:

Steve Phillips
Sandy Ogsbury
Bruce Brown
Joan Brown
Mark Sadan
Amalie Rothschild
Arnold Leo
Charlotte Louise Farrugia
Ann Wakefield
Donald Gangemi
Jo Gangemi
Carol Launer
Christine Harvey

contents

creative film-making

1

the illusion of motion

The mind tries very hard to make sense of the world. When confronted with sensory data the mind tries to find a pattern or a design relating the pieces of data to each other. This insistence on finding meaningful patterns or designs, even in very random data, is one of the major reasons why motion pictures seem to move.

Let us examine one of the simplest possible cases. In a dark room we see a yellow light on the opposite wall. It goes out, but at the same time another identical light goes on two feet to the right of the first. Now, if the left and right lights alternate being on at a steady and fairly rapid rate, we will soon have the sensation that there is only one light involved, and that it is moving very rapidly back and forth at regular intervals. My theory of how the mind goes about setting up this illusion is this: Since both lights are identical it is simpler to think of them as one light, thus reducing the number of factors to be fit into a pattern. But since this light appears in two different positions, it must be moving back and forth to get to those positions. The notion of the light moving back and forth is really much simpler than the notion of two lights going off and on at exactly opposite times in relation to each other. Notice that even the verbal explanation of the two-light setup is much more complicated than the explanation of the single light moving back and forth. To create the illusion of movement, in this case, may well be the quickest, easiest for the mind to make a pattern of the sensory data of the lights.

A reel of motion-picture film contains a very large number of still photographs. When we see these projected onto a screen in very rapid succession, the illusion that the images are moving is overwhelmingly real. This illusion is often attributed to the physiological phenomenon of persistence of vision, but this in itself is quite unable to account for our thinking we see motion; it only accounts for our being unaware of the blank screen between each successive frame of the movie. The reason that we *think* we see motion is to be found in the mind, not in the eye. We are presented with a situation very much like that of the two yellow lights, and our mental reaction to it is quite similar. Let us suppose the movie we are looking at now is of an Indian shooting an arrow at a bear. The first still photograph of the Indian shows him holding the bow with arrow pulled back. The next still photograph projected onto the screen is identical, except that the arrow has moved (moved?) one inch forward on its flight. The third photograph is identical, except that now the arrow is in a position two inches ahead of where it was in the first photograph. Twenty-four photographs later the arrow is in a position just touching the bear. The standard amount of time taken to project all of these still photographs in a motion-picture theater is one second. We could, perhaps, think of what we have seen as 24 pictures, each with an arrow in a different position, but that would be taking reality at face value, without trying to

The illusion of motion is created by the mind interpreting the successive changes of image position.

find order and simplicity in it. It is much neater to think of what we have seen as a single photograph with a single arrow *Moving* across it toward the bear. It is also a lot more fun.

The mechanics of the projection and perception of film are interesting in themselves, but they have even more importance in relation to creative possibilities in film, which will be explored in following chapters. For this reason it is important to know the basic mechanics.

The standard number of frames (still photographs) projected onto the screen in motion-picture theaters all over the world is 24 per second. This frame rate was arrived at by experience with how fast the pictures had to be replaced in order to make the illusion smooth, and how fast the sound track on the film had to pass in order to get reasonable sound fidelity. In order to maintain lower costs for those making home movies, the standard frame-per-second rate for amateur equipment has been set at 18 frames per second (a recent revision from the former 16 per second). Films which are to have an integrated sound track and be shown either in theaters or on television must be photographed at the rate of 24 frames per second.

When we see a two-hour film, we have actually been looking at a blank screen for a total of nearly an hour. The explanation for this is that while the film is running, each successive frame is pulled into position for projection by a claw, and then left stationary while the projector's light beam projects it onto the screen. Then a shutter blocks off the beam during the time it takes to pull the next frame into position. Thus the light beam is blocked to hide the view of the next frame being brought into position. However, since screen flicker occuring at the rate of 24 times per second is objectionable, the shutter is designed to interrupt the light beam three times during the time each stationary frame is being projected. Although this causes more flickers per second, the subjective effect is one of smoother continuity.

When the projector shutter cuts off the beam of light to the screen, we do not immediately cease to see the image of the frame that was just there. The retinal surface of our eyes continues to remain excited by the image for about a thirtieth of a second. Since we are projecting subsequent frames at a faster rate than that, the after image (persistence of vision) does not have time to disappear entirely before the image of the next frame takes its place, and we therefore don't perceive the blank screen between frames. During the projection of the 172,800 frames of a two-hour film, the projector shutter has been closed for a total of about one hour, and during that time we have been seeing only our retinal afterimages.

2

film stock formats

Most of the films you see were photographed and projected in a film size 35 millimeters wide. This film is of the same dimensions as 35mm still-camera film. But since the film runs vertically through a motion-picture camera, rather than horizontally as in a still camera, the individual frames of a 35mm theatrical film are less than half the size of a 35mm color slide—yet they must be projected onto screens that are from forty to sixty feet wide. This demands a very high degree of precision in optics and mechanical registration from both cameras and projectors, and is part of the reason why motion-picture equipment is so expensive.

For large-budget extravaganza films the 70mm format has been used in recent years. Using a film stock this wide means that a very large screen can be filled with very good photographic fidelity. Most of the special film presentations at recent World's Fairs have been presented in this format. Using a film stock this wide also affords room alongside the edge for more than one optical sound track, so that it is quite feasible to have different parts of the sound come from different parts of the theater, or—to have stereophonic sound.

There are several interesting variations on the 35mm format for theatrical films. One of the most ambitious was Cinerama, in which three cameras running simultaneously could film a scene of very wide dimensions, each camera covering one-third the angle of view. To screen this required three projectors running in synchronization, each covering one third of a very wide screen area. The overlap between the sections was always visible and distracting, and the whole setup, while a great novelty, was very clumsy and expensive.

The first great improvement in wide-screen presentation was Cinemascope, which made use of a very ingenious lens design which can "squeeze" an image horizontally to half its normal size, and thus only one camera can record a very wide view on the standard-size 35mm film. A special lens is then used on the projector which "unsqueezes" the image, and the resulting image is twice the screen width of the normal 35mm lens system.

An important new variation on the 35mm gauge is the Techniscope format. This uses standard 35mm film, but forms images of only half the normal height. Thus the ratio of height to width is about two to one, and is directly suitable for wide-screen presentation. By various methods of reproduction, a film shot in the Techniscope format can be printed into at least eight different release-print forms, including 16mm prints, prints for television, standard prints, wide-screen prints, and even 70mm prints. Also, since each frame is only half as high as normal, film runs through the camera at only half the rate, effecting substantial cost reductions during shooting. Many 35mm cameras are now being built or modified to shoot in the Techniscope format.

The 16mm format was designed originally as an inexpensive film size for home movies. The quality was poor, and the equipment available for 16mm was rather crude. During World War II there was a tremendous need for training and propaganda films. Since 16mm was so much smaller, lighter, cheaper and more portable than 35mm, it was utilized in great quantities, and for the first time some effort was made to engineer equipment that would be rugged and capable. Business, industry, education, medicine and Government started using the 16mm format extensively. Then television networks began shooting many of their documentary specials in 16mm, as well as their news footage. Most of the serious "underground," experimental and independent film-makers work in 16mm, and increasing numbers of film festivals are being established that feature 16mm production. According to Eastman Kodak Company the sale of 16mm film stock exceeds in total screen time any of the other gauges.

As film emulsions were improved, it became feasible to market an even smaller gauge, 8mm film, for home movie use. The technical improvements in 8mm cameras and projectors have been significant. Combined with the new high-quality color film stocks, the projection quality is quite satisfactory for small showings. However 8mm is now being replaced by Super 8, which, happily, is one of those highly touted improvements that actually turns out to be a lot better. Super 8 is still 8 millimeters wide, but because the sprocket hole is in a vertical shape, the picture width on the 8mm strip can be made wider. At the same time the height is increased proportionately, and the resultant area of each frame is about 50 per cent greater, resulting in better image and color quality, as well as allowing more light to reach the screen for a brighter image. Sound-on-film systems for Super 8 are in the trial stages; but it is only a matter of time before its quality and versatility levels will reach those required for commercial distribution and Super 8 will join 16mm as a gauge that started out for home use and then became useful for professional purposes.

In the 35mm gauge, 90 feet of film run through the projector per minute; in 16mm, 36 feet per minute are run through; in Super 8, 14.8 feet are passed per minute, and in regular 8mm the rate is 13.5 feet per minute.

Standard 35mm, 16mm, Super 8, and 8mm.

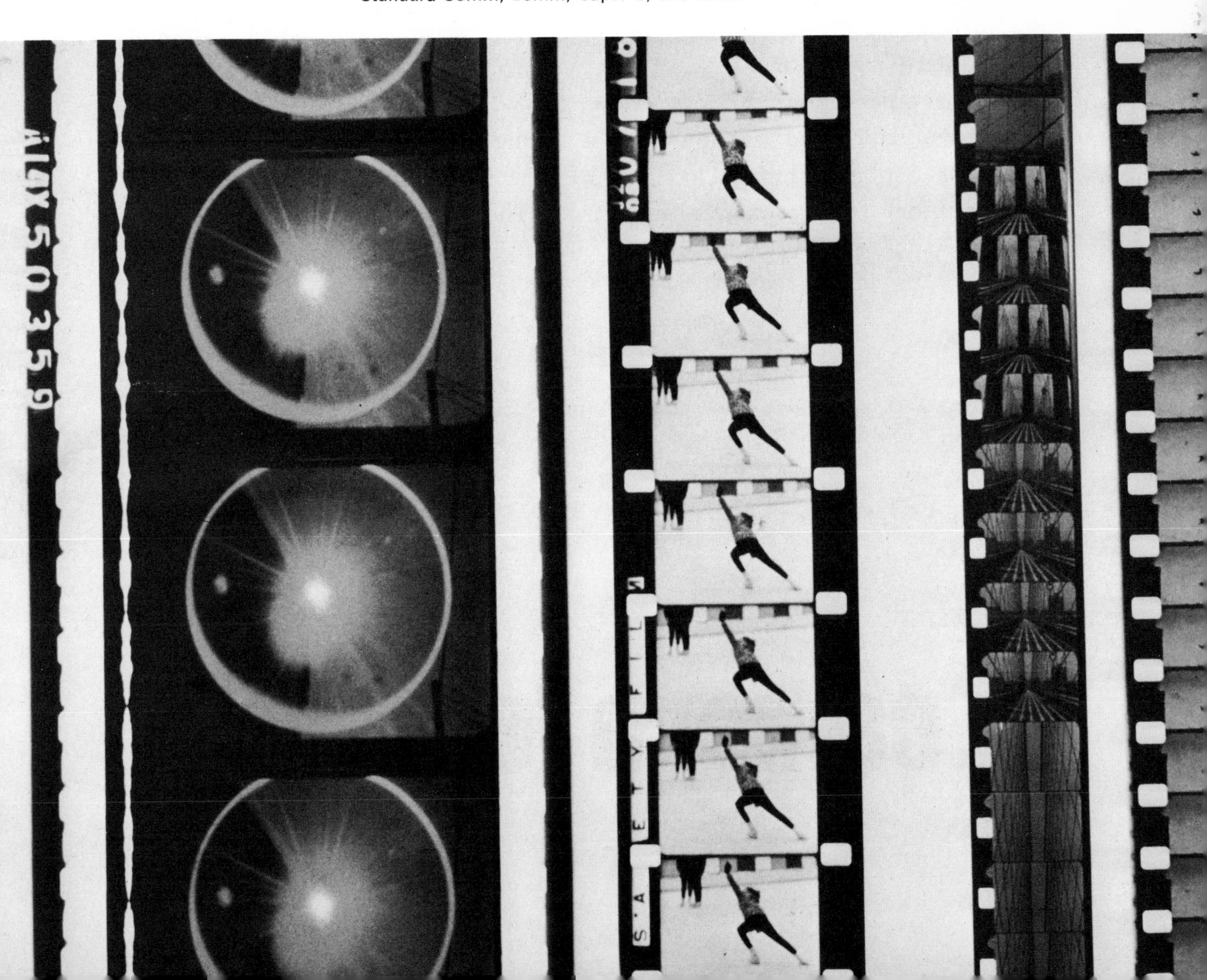

3

By far the most important feature of any motion-picture camera is the viewfinding system. The ideal viewfinder would, of course, show us the image as it would appear on the projection screen. The nearest thing to this at the present state of technology is the true reflex finder. There are two basic ways of making it possible to see through the viewfinder the image actually formed by the taking lens. One is to insert a partial reflection mirror into the image beam just before it reaches the camera shutter. This mirror will reflect about 16 per cent of the light into the viewfinding optics, and yet allow the rest to pass straight through to the film emulsion. Thus, whatever the lens sees will be shown in the viewfinder, and when you focus the lens on an object you will see the image in the viewfinder likewise come into focus. Since the reflecting mirror is located in front of the opening and closing shutter, there is no flicker in the viewfinder as the camera runs. As the lens opening is changed, the image in the viewfinder will get dimmer or brighter. The 16 per cent loss of light to the film surface because of the diversion to the viewfinder has only a very slight effect on the exposure of the film.

The other method of reflex viewing involves the use of a shutter which has its front surface mirrored. The beam of light from the lens

camera features

passes directly to the film surface when the shutter is open, but when it closes, interrupting the beam, the mirrored surface reflects the image into the viewfinder. Thus the light image is directed alternately onto the film and into the viewfinder. In this way 100 per cent of the light goes into the viewfinder, making a brighter image than the partial-mirror system does; but the image, in this case, flickers as the shutter opens and closes, and thus there is, in effect, only about 50 per cent light transmission.

A true reflex system makes the camera tremendously versatile, and also gives assurance at the time of shooting that you are actually getting what you are seeing. It enables the cameraman to see directly the effects of using special prisms, filters and special lenses, and to change focus from one object to another during a shot without previous rehearsal. When we explore other elements of film making in later chapters, the tremendous value of the reflex system will become even more apparent.

Most professional cameras are driven by electric motors. There are two major types of motors available, and professional cameras are built to use either one interchangeably. When you are shooting silent footage, you need the versatility of a variable-speed motor, so that you can make slow-motion and accelerated-motion shots. When you are shooting synchronous sound footage, some kind of "sync" motor is required. If you are shooting where standard AC power is available, the easiest thing to do is use a sync motor which runs at exactly 24 frames per second by relating to the 60-cycle pulses of the AC power. This is the same principle by which an electric clock keeps ac-

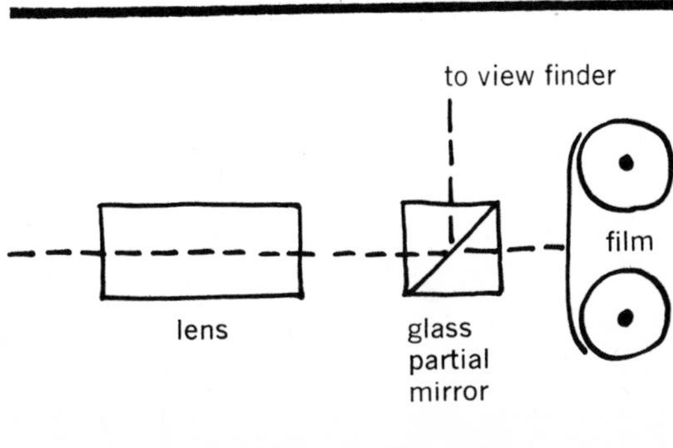

Beam-splitter reflex

curate time. If you are shooting out in the field and must run the camera on battery power (which has no built-in 60-cycle timing pulse), then a transistorized timing device must be used. These will be explained clearly in the chapter on synchronizing sound to picture.

It is probably apparent at this point that what kind of camera and accessories you use depends on what the specifics are of the film you are making. It is frequently the case that different cameras are used for different parts of a film. Let us imagine some situations that will arise in a hypothetical film we are making and see what camera features we will need. The title of our film requires letters to assemble themselves into the various words, so we will need a camera that can take a single frame at a time; and between each taking of a frame we will move the letters a little bit by hand into the positions we want. Then a boy and girl are talking and we must hear their words synchronized to their lip movements, so we need a camera that will run at *exactly* 24 frames per second, and that also will not make any *noise* while it is running, since this would mar the sound recording of the conversation. Then there is a shot of the interior of a cathedral where there is not enough light for a good exposure; bringing in lights is out of the question, so for this we need a camera that will not only take single frames at a time but will allow the shutter to be held open long enough to get enough exposure on each frame. Following this scene is one where the shot starts out on a large yellow daisy, then the focus changes very smoothly to the girl in the field ten feet farther away, and then she slips out of focus and a figure is seen

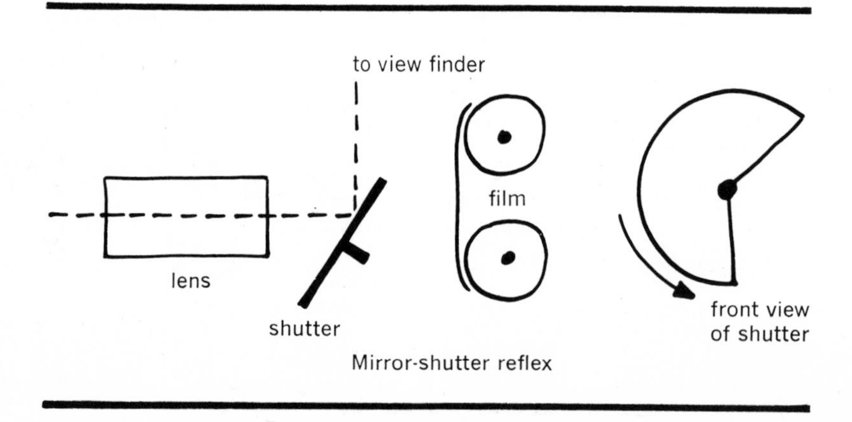

Mirror-shutter reflex

in a tree beyond her. For this we clearly need a true reflex viewfinder to see what the focus is doing, and a camera capable of accepting a very long telephoto lens. Then comes the long continuous shot where the camera takes the place of the person's eyes and runs along the sidewalk, into a tall building, gets into an elevator, goes to the top floor, and walks into an executive office for a confrontation. This requires a camera which will accept an oversize magazine of film so that the film will not run out in the middle of the shot; an automatic-exposure system would be very good here in addition, since the light levels will vary greatly, and trying to change exposure manually while running with the camera is going to be very difficult. Our final scene is of ocean waves breaking in slow motion on a purple beach, and during this shot a closeup of a single human eye fades into a superimposition upon the wave scene and then slowly fades away. For the slow-motion effect to be pronounced, a camera running speed of at least 48 frames per second will be required. The beach may be made purple by means of a gelatin filter of that color, which on some cameras can be inserted behind the lens in a special slot. For the eye to materialize as a superimposed image requires three features. First, the camera has to allow for winding the film of the waves back to the starting point so that the eye shot can be double-exposed onto it. Second, in order for the eye to gradually appear and to fade away smoothly, a variable shutter is required which can smoothly increase the amount of exposure from nothing to full and then back again. Third, the camera must be one in which the normal lens can be taken off and a special macro lens substituted for such an extreme closeup.

Some professional cameras are equipped with mechanisms known as registration pins. These are extremely close tolerance pins which engage each frame by the sprocket holes *after* the transport claw has pulled that frame into shooting position. Thus, each frame is held rock-steady during its exposure, and each frame is held in precisely the same position as the previous one. For general-purpose work, registration pins are not required, as the frames are positioned with sufficient accuracy by the claw-transport mechanism. Registration pins are desirable when the type of multiple exposure to be made in the camera requires that the alignment between elements in the first exposure and the second exposure cannot be allowed to vary, however slightly.

Following are the cameras most often used for professional film work in the United States, along with comments on their special features and their approximate cost. Almost all of this equipment can be rented from suppliers in major cities.

The standard camera of the 35mm theatrical industry is the Mitchell BNC. It runs silently, can now be obtained with reflex viewing, has a variable shutter, can run at speeds up to 128 frames per second, has provision for interchangeable motors and lenses, has registration pins which hold each frame absolutely steady during its exposure, will run backward, accepts different-sized magazines of film, and has a huge range of accessories available for special purposes. It is a very large camera, too heavy for one man to lift. Prices run above $20,000. It can be rented for about $100 per day.

Mitchell 35mm camera, model BNC-VTR Reflex. The Sony TV pickup will send the viewfinder image to a video-tape recorder, thus providing instant replay of scenes just shot. *(Courtesy F&B/Ceco, Inc.)*

Arriflex 35mm camera, model 35 11c, showing sync pulse circuit inside. *(Courtesy Arriflex Corporation, Inc.)*

Mitchell cameras are also available in non-silent and non-reflex versions for about $30 per day.

For silent shooting in 35mm a great favorite is the Arriflex 35, which features, above all, hand-held portability. It can be run from a battery pack worn as a belt, has mirror shutter reflex viewing, variable running speeds, a three-lens turret, interchangeable motors, will not normally run backward, can be obtained with a variable shutter, and can be fitted with an accessory single-frame motor. The price is about $3,000, plus lenses. Rentals are about $25 per day.

There are various models of Bell and Howell 35mm cameras available, and perhaps the most unusual of any of them is the old "Eyemo" combat camera, which takes 100-foot rolls of film and can be easily held in one hand. This has no fancy features, but its small size can sometimes be very useful. Rental is about $10 per day.

The range of 16mm cameras in use is quite wide. For portable sound shooting an excellent choice is the Eclair NPR. This camera runs very quietly (not silently), is designed for hand-held shooting, has mirror-reflex viewing of very high quality, has a two-lens turret, interchangeable motors for battery or AC operation, a viewing eyepiece that will swivel in several directions, making unusual angle shots much easier, 400-foot magazines, a semivariable shutter (this cannot be operated during camera running), automatic clapper system and sync pulse generator for faster and easier sound shooting, magazines can be changed in five seconds for minimum delay during fast-breaking action; it also has a very low profile without the usual Mickey Mouse ears type of magazine on top

Bell & Howell 35mm Eyemo camera, custom fitted with a beam splitter reflex viewing system. *(Courtesy F&B/Ceco, Inc.)*

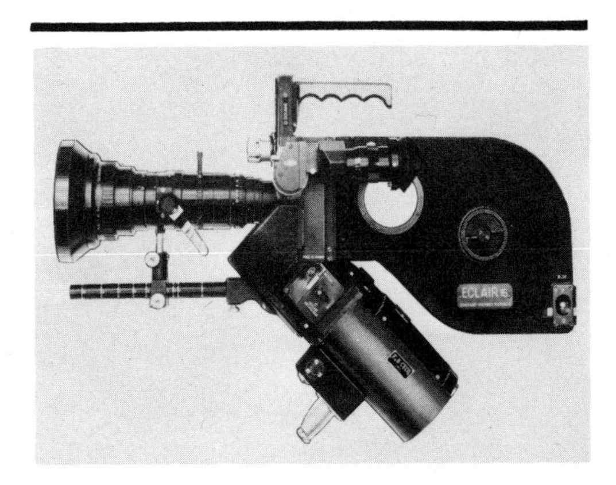

Eclair 16mm noiseless camera, fitted with a zoom lens. *(Courtesy F&B/Ceco, Inc.)*

of the camera. Price is about $4,800, without lenses. Rental is about $50 per day.

One of the most versatile cameras is the Bolex Reflex 16. This camera uses the partial mirror or "beam splitter" type of reflex viewing, has a built-in and extremely reliable spring-powered motor, will run at speeds from 12 to 64 frames per second, has a variable shutter for fades and dissolves, a single-frame release, film windback with a frame counter to keep accurate track of where you are on the film, time exposure of single frames built in, and it will accept a sync pulse battery-powered motor for sound shooting. The Rex V model has a 400-foot magazine. The camera is very compact, weighing about six pounds. Prices with a set of three lenses on the turret run about $1,000. Rental is around $15 per day.

An even lighter camera is the Beaulieu R-16 Auto. It weighs about five pounds and is battery operated by a motor that compares its own running speed to an accurate standard provided by a transistor circuit in the camera—any variations are self corrected. The camera has a mirror-shutter-reflex viewing system, an automatic-exposure system that reads the amount of light falling on the viewfinder ground glass for extremely versatile exposure control under unusual conditions. The camera will take 200-foot accessory magazines and has a built-in sync pulse generator for sound shooting. It will run at speeds of two to 64 frames per second. Price, with three lenses on the turret, is about $1,400.

One of the most widely used cameras is the Arriflex 16 S. It has mirror-shutter-reflex viewing, a three-lens turret featuring quick-change lens mounts, interchangeable motors,

Bolex 16mm reflex, model Rex V, fitted with an automatic exposure control zoom lens, and with a mount for a 400-foot film magazine on top of the camera. *(Courtesy Paillard, Inc.)*

Bolex 16mm Pro, a radical new camera for sync sound shooting. *(Courtesy Paillard, Inc.)*

registration-pin movement, a tachometer for direct reading of the actual running speed (which can be varied between 0 and 50 frames per second), a frame counter, is able to run backward, will accept 400-foot magazines, and weighs about eight pounds with lenses. With one motor and three lenses, the price is about $3,000. Rental is about $20 per day.

Arriflex also makes a special quiet camera for sync sound shooting, the 16 BL. It comes complete with a wide-range zoom lens, sync pulse generator and, on special order, a variable shutter for dissolves. The price for this camera is a little under $5,000. Rental is about $55 per day.

For network news filming, cameras made by the Auricon Company are often used. These cameras are capable of recording sound along the edge of the film, instead of requiring a separate recording machine as do the other cameras described. This method of recording sound is called single-system, and is useful in recording speeches, and interviews of which there will be virtually no later editing done. For use in more complex types of film, where there is dramatic dialogue and where freedom of editing choice in picture and sound relationship is required, this type of camera is totally unsuitable, due to limited fidelity of the sound, and due to the fact that recording picture and sound on the same strip of material makes it impossible to edit them independently. Auricons are very often converted to double-system operation (separate camera and recorder) and improved with the addition of 400-foot film magazine, quieter running gears, special motors, etc. The basic camera does not have reflex viewing, but is usually used with a zoom lens containing its own

Beaulieu 16mm reflex, model R16B auto, fitted with a zoom lens and a 200-foot accessory film magazine. *(Courtesy Cinema Beaulieu, Inc.)*

Arriflex 16S, fitted with a matte box in front of the lens. *(Courtesy of Arriflex Corporation, Inc.)*

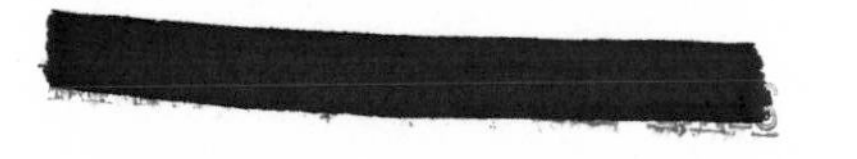

viewing optics. The cost of a basic Auricon with improvements needed to make it a fully professional camera range between $2,000 and $3,000. Rental of such is about $35 per day.

Few 8mm cameras these days are designed for versatility. The person who wants to use 8mm as a serious medium of exploration and visual expression will be frustrated by the degree to which 8mm cameras are automated. Therefore the Fujica Z-2 is welcome, because it allows for considerable visual manipulation. It features semireflex viewing using a split-image rangefinder in a through-the-lens viewfinding system. It has a high-quality zoom lens, an automatic-exposure system with manual override, a variable shutter for fades, a rewind facility for running the film back in order to make multiple exposures. This camera will accept only the film cartridge made by Fujica, which, unlike the Kodak cartridge, allows for winding the film back for making dissolves and multiple exposures. The Fujica Z-2 costs under $200.

Bolex makes a Super 8 camera, the Model 155, which incorporates an incredible new zoom lens capable of focus from infinity to as close as one inch. The previous limit of similar lenses had been about four feet. With such unusual closeup ability, this camera is an especially good tool for films that must show small detail clearly, such as laboratory processes, architects' models, dental techniques, biological specimens, and the like. With this camera a closeup of a penny filling the entire screen is quite easily filmed. The viewfinding system is semireflex, using a rangefinder superimposed on the through-the-lens viewing system. The camera uses the Kodak Super 8 cartridge.

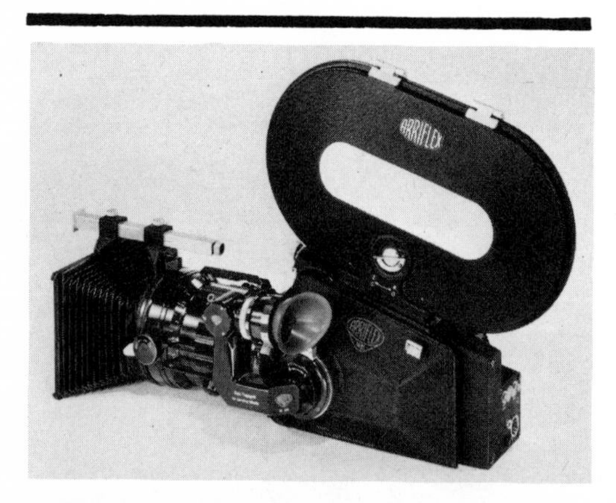

Arriflex 16BL, a noiseless 16mm camera, fitted with a matte box and a 400 foot magazine. *(Courtesy Arriflex Corporation, Inc.)*

Auricon Cine-Voice 16mm camera after extensive modification. A crystal circuit controls the running speed exactly at 24 fps. *(Courtesy F&B/Ceco, Inc.)*

List price i…   recorder automatically starts.
B…   g projection the tape recorder is
soun…   d into the projector, and pic-
lizes   sound are presented in sync.
whose   for camera, recorder, and
camera.   s about $450.

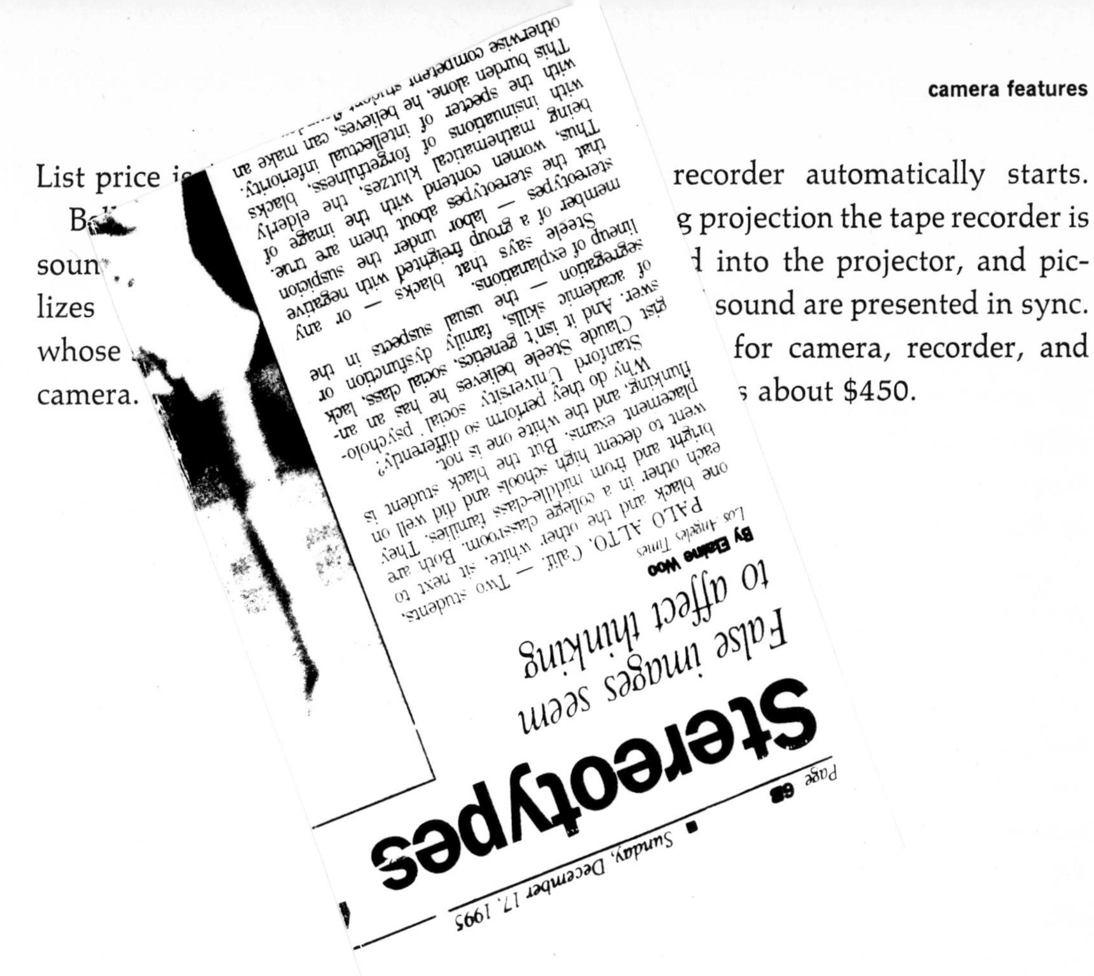

Sunday, December 17, 1995

Page 6B

Stereotypes

False images seem to affect thinking

By Elaine Woo
Los Angeles Times

PALO ALTO, Calif. — Two students, one black and the other white, sit next to each other in a college classroom. Both are bright and from middle-class families. They went to decent high schools and did well on placement exams. But the black student is flunking, and the white one is not.

Why do they perform so differently?

Stanford University social psychologist Claude Steele believes he has an answer. And it isn't genetics, social class, lack of academic skills, family dysfunction or segregation — the usual suspects in the lineup of explanations.

Steele says that blacks — or any member of a group freighted with negative stereotypes — labor under the suspicion that the stereotypes about them are true. Thus, women contend with the image of being mathematical klutzes, the elderly with insinuations of forgetfulness, blacks with the specter of intellectual inferiority. This burden alone, he believes, can make an otherwise competent student

Fujica Z2, a Super 8 camera.

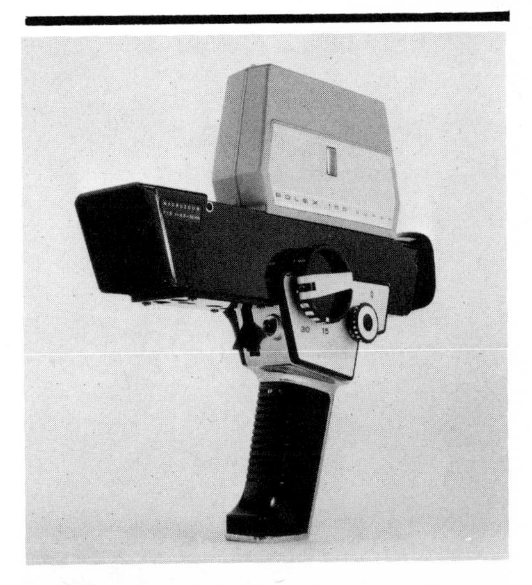

Bolex 155 equipped with a macro zoom lens.

4

lighting

It often happens that the natural play of light on a scene before us is quite beautiful. Perhaps it is a sailboat heading into a mist, or beams of sunlight filtering down through tall trees, or candlelight on a girl's face, or the pattern of highlight and shadow on the side of an old barn. Each of these scenes is visible only because of the light it reflects and is photographable only by that light. Thus it makes sense to think of the objects in a scene as modifiers of light, and not so much as objects in themselves. This seeming complication in regarding the visible world is really a simplification enabling the film-maker to deal more deftly with his images. To the sailor the sail is many yards of canvas, to the film-maker it is just as readily a white triangle, because when he photographs it that's all he will get on film—no canvas, just a white shape. This has meaning in relation to what shapes will follow in succeeding scenes and in relation to how a double-exposed image will photograph on top of the sailboat scene, and in the present instance it opens the thinking as to how we will light this sailboat scene. Our lighting unit in this case is the sun, and we need to figure out where we want to put it. We might well start the shot with the camera looking up at the sail against the sky, with the sunlight coming over from behind the camera. This would yield an opaque white sail. By bringing the sun around toward the front of the boat while the camera is still running, we will cause the sail to darken gradually as the side toward the camera becomes shaded. By continuing to bring the sun around behind the sail so that it glows through the sail and is seen by the camera, we have a fairly dark sail with a very diffused, hazy, dim sun moving across it. If we now get a shot of the sailboat entering into the bank of mist (shot from another boat) we will have a very good visual sequence comprising a bright, white sail against the blue sky, changing smoothly into a darker sail, with a diffused and misty white sun moving across the sail texture, and finally, the diffused white sailboat itself moving into the mist. In this case the lighting of the scene is what gives it most of its value. The movement of the sun is accomplished by smoothly turning the boat a half circle so that it ends up going in the opposite direction. But the shot itself does not show this, since the sail is shown only against the sky.

Now let us consider a scene of a few people sitting in the grass on a bright, sunny day. We want to film them in such a way as to flatter their looks and to make the scene look very pretty and pleasant. As we look at these people, we notice that those facing the sun are illuminated in a glaring and flat-surfaced way. Those turned away from the sun have their faces in deep shadow. And finally, the faces of those at right angles to the sun are bright on one side and dark on the other. The scene as it is will not photograph as we want it at all. As we look, with the camera, at the faces turned

Direct sunlight without any diffusion.

Side light with no fill light for the shadow side of the face.

Back lighting with no fill on the face.

By putting a diffusion scrim into the light path the shadows are softened and the skin tone is mellowed.

The shadow can be filled with a reflector for a more pleasing balance.

By using a reflector the skin tone can be improved and catch light put in the eyes.

toward the sun, the first thing that happens is the loss of three-dimensionality, since the camera has only one eye. This causes the faces to blend in with the background and thus lose their sense of specialness. Also, because there are no shadows on the front-lit faces, they look flat, as though cut of paper. The whole effect of a shot like this is visually banal or plain-looking. To improve this shot we need to diffuse the sunlight hitting the faces so that the skin tone will be more glowing and less glary. A yard or two of sheer white nylon held in the path of the sun's rays a few feet from the subjects will take care of this.

Now let's look at the faces turned away from the sun. The camera eye, because of the characteristics of the film stock itself, will have difficulty in seeing any detail at all in the shaded face. If we increase the exposure in order to bring out detail, the area of the shot around the face, which is in bright sunlight, will be washed out from overexposure. What we need to do is reduce the contrast between the shadowed face and the bright background. This can be done by reflecting sunlight onto the face in shadow, by means of a reflector. These can be rented or purchased, but they can also be homemade. Cover a piece of stiff cardboard with household aluminum foil, placing the dull, matte side of the foil on the surface. A reflector two or three feet square will throw an amazing amount of light. The direct sunlight coming from above and behind the head of the subject, gives a very good-looking "rim light," which shows off the sheen of the hair and outlines the head for good background separation.

The faces at right angles to the sun

need some reflected light to fill in the shadow sides, and perhaps some diffusion of the direct sunlight on the bright sides.

With these modifications, the quality of the images of the people undergoes an amazing change for the better. The shots become a sensual pleasure to look at, and give a feeling of grace and beauty. The effort involved in making these improvements is very small, and the aesthetic reward great.

In feature film production, it is more common to use arc lights than reflectors, and special silks instead of nylon. But arc lights require heavy-duty DC generators to run them and trained men to operate the equipment, so shortcuts such as the reflector are much appreciated on small-budget productions.

Once we move indoors where electric power is readily available, the kinds of lighting effects possible enlarge considerably. The first thing to do is notice where the light already in an interior is coming from. If, for the most part, you like the effect that it gives but measure it as insufficient for good exposure, you can boost it with small lighting units that throw light in the same direction as the natural source, and thus get plenty of exposure without spoiling the original effect. Let us suppose there are a couple of large table lamps with large lampshades. We can take out the bulbs and replace them temporarily with 500-watt photoflood bulbs. These cost about a dollar apiece. They will only burn for about three or four hours, but that is a small price to pay for a light output of roughly ten times as much as the normal household bulb. The next thing to do is figure where the people in the scene will be sitting or standing. Then you can put up a small rim light for each one. This back-light effect is the same as we got in the outdoor sequence. The lighting unit itself should be put up on the wall behind the person being filmed, and usually as high up as possible so that it won't be seen by the camera. In cases where a person in the scene is not near enough to one of the modified photoflood lamps, we will need a lighting unit aimed at them. If this light comes from the direction of the nearest photoflood table lamp, then it will appear to be the light from the lamp itself, and thus the natural effect can be maintained. When a person is moving around from one lit place in the room to another, it may not be necessary to use additional lights because there is probably enough illumination spilling from the sources and bouncing around the room for adequate exposure. There is no need to flood an entire scene with a full-exposure level of light. Doing so actually makes the scene less interesting to look at. As the people move from area to area of light, the eye is entertained as they move through the shadow in between.

Although there are no formulas for lighting scenes, some general approaches can be described. It is important to place the lighting units high off the floor. This accomplishes several things at once. It creates a shadow pattern on faces that tends to be flattering, since the eye sockets are in slight shadow, the cheekbones are highlighted, the mouth is modeled by slight shadow, and the shadow created by the nose is kept short and downward on the face. At the same time, since the lights are well above eye level of the actors, the problem of the lights' causing them to squint is minimized. If the lights are high up toward the ceiling, they will not often be in the camera's field of view; this allows much more freedom of camera angle with a given light setup. There is also the advantage of a single lighting unit's doing the work of two in some cases, since a main light shining on one actor can also provide rim lighting for an actor facing him.

In black-and-white photography it is traditional to use three lighting units for a person. The main light comes from in front of the person and somewhat to one side. This provides the chief illumination and, because it is toward one side of the face and figure, gives a three-dimensional modeling. The shadow side of the face and figure is illuminated just enough to show surface detail in the shadow areas caused by the main light. This light is called a fill light, and may be a half or a third as bright as the main light. The third light used is a rim light, which shines from behind and above the actor. This, especially in the case of blondes, gives a highlight sheen to the hair, and an edge of light delineating the head from the background.

Lighting for color shooting is in some ways easier than for black and white, because the differences in color of subjects and their backgrounds help to give them spatial separation. A favorable lighting setup for faces is the use of the very diffused main source from up high and roughly 45 degrees to either side of the camera, then a bright "kicker" light from behind to the opposite side of the head. This gives three-dimensional modeling and a bright edge delineating one side of the face.

Architectural details such as brick walls, mantels, door frames, paneled walls, etc., can best be shown off by a light source placed so that the beam skims along the surface creating textures of light and shadow to emphasize the details of the surface being skimmed. A very good use of this technique would be in lighting a beamed ceiling with a light aimed at right angles to the camera-lens axis, and just touching the lower surfaces of each of the beams, thus creating contrasting shadows that cause the beams to stand out strongly.

Sometimes the film-maker is confronted with what seems like an impossible situation to light well. He needs to put light in certain places in the scene but there seems to be no way to get it there without the lighting unit itself showing obtrusively in the picture. The solution is clever hiding of lighting units within the scene, placed so that they can not be seen by the camera. A good example is that of a large factory interior in which a chase sequence is to occur. If it is desired to have light only in certain key areas of the action, and if many of the shots will be in wide angle, showing the rear wall and the walls at each side, then hiding the lights in the scene would be the only feasible solution. The lighting units can be placed behind air ducts, behind vertical columns, behind packing crates; and, in cases where there is no convenient spot to hide a unit, you can always put a suitable prop into the scene and then put a light behind that. Many a time a large book or vase has been placed on a desk for no other reason than this. In some cases the lights may appear in the scene without messing it up. For example, a string of small lights along the ceiling of a mine shaft would seem quite normal to an audience. Or, large spotlights on the deck

The three light sources illuminating this scene are all within the camera's field of view.

of a Coast Guard patrol boat would seem quite normal. It is surprising how often a motion-picture lighting unit can be put in a scene right where you want it and still not call attention to itself. Documentary cameramen who have to make do with shortcuts become quite adept at this sort of game.

Lighting such areas as hallways and stairways can seem very difficult at first, but it is actually very easy and often yields striking images. If the shot looks down a long hallway (we will assume there are doors along the hall), shining a bright light down the hall will yield terrible results. The hall will look flat, rather than giving a sense of depth, and the area closest to the camera will be vastly overexposed, while the far end of the hall will be underexposed. The usual solution would be to open a few of the doors, put lighting units in the rooms, and aim them through the doorways out into the hall. In this way lights can be placed along the length of the hallway without their being seen. As a person walks toward the camera from the far end of the hall, he will pass through these beams and be illuminated by the cross-light—which gives good modeling. The exposure of the figure will be constant in each of the beams, regardless of which end of the hall it is in, and the movement of the figure through the beams is much more interesting than it would be in flat light. The same lighting solution can be applied to shooting in stairwells; a stairwell can be considered a vertical hallway.

Many film sequences purportedly take place in the dark. How can you set up a scene so that it looks dark, or least like nighttime, and still be able to have it register on photo-

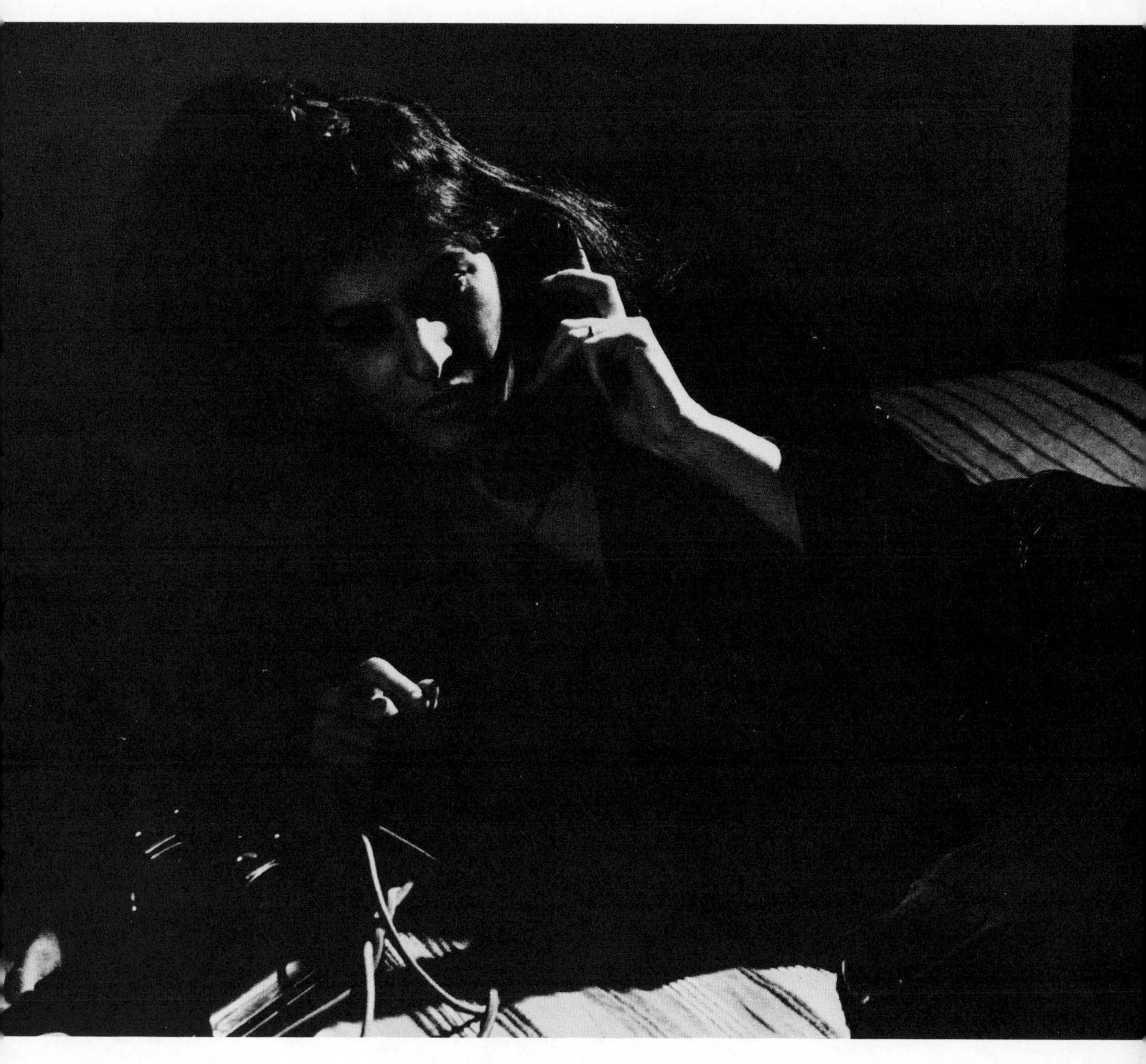

By lighting only the edge of the figure the scene may be interpreted as occurring in near darkness.

Surface textures revealed by the raking sunlight.

graphic film? The secret is to use rim lighting only; the outlines of a figure may then be clearly seen against the black background, and yet, since there is virtually no light on the surface of the figure, the audience will think of the scene as being quite dark. Usually a figure will be lit from both left and right sides with the lighting units placed well behind the subject so that only the edge of the figure shows any illumination. In a closeup, we must, of course, provide a little light to make facial expression visible, and the method for making this possible is to use the same rim lighting technique on the head, and set the illumination level on the face so that there is only about 25 per cent of normal exposure. This will be explained in Chapter 6.

The equipment needed for lighting in professional film work varies between an aluminum reflector, as a minimum, and several truckloads full of gear as a maximum. There have been some very welcome recent improvements in lighting technology. Preeminent among these is the development of the tungsten-halogen lamp bulb. This bulb is about the size of your finger and operates in a unique way. In an ordinary lamp, as the tungsten filament glows, the surface of the tungsten evaporates and is deposited on the inside surface of the glass, causing it to become darkened. The loss of tungsten from the filament soon withers it away and the bulb burns out. In the new bulb the tungsten redeposits itself onto the filament, so the bulb envelope remains clear and efficient, and the filament is able to glow at extremely high temperatures without quickly burning out. An ordinary glass bulb subjected to such a high temperature would soon melt, so "quartz" or special glass is used instead. The saving in total size of a lighting unit using these bulbs is dramatic. A "quartz" unit consuming 650 watts puts out as much light as a standard bulb consuming 2,000 watts, and the size of the whole unit is about one fifth the older one.

Smith-Victor Corporation makes a set of three "quartz" lighting heads, each with a lightweight collapsible stand, and all fitting inside a single attaché-sized case, for $100.

The most popular "quartz" lights are those made by Colortran Industries. Their general-purpose 650-watt unit is priced at about $34. The Colortran Super-Beam 1000 uses a 1,000-watt bulb and features variable focusing of the beam from spot to flood. For even lighting of large surfaces with a minimum of shadow the Colortran Soft Lite units are available in wattages from 750 to 4,000 watts, at prices starting at $80. For use in smooth filling of shadow areas they make a "broad" in various wattages at prices from $60. Rentals for these units are about $2 per day (you supply the bulbs). For those situations where there is no place to plug in light sources, Sylvania makes a battery-powered Sun Gun unit that will run for about a half hour before it needs recharging. The complete unit rents for about $7 a day.

One of the least expensive ways of lighting small-area location jobs is to use R40 photo-reflector bulbs (available from photography stores) in conjunction with Lowell-Light hardware. The basic unit is a porcelain socket, swivel-mounted on a small metal plate, which has various notches cut into it so that it is easy to hang onto a nail or a pipe or a door edge—in fact, almost any kind of protuberance. If none of these is available, the unit may even be stuck onto a flat surface with heavy-duty tape, because it is so light. These features make it very versatile and allow you to put lights up all over a room without having to bring any stands along with you; and the problem of keeping light stands out of view of your shots is thus avoided. The basic socket unit costs about $6 each, the bulb about $2, and there is a complete line of accessories available.

A most useful accessory on a lighting unit is a set of "barn doors." These are hinged flaps on the sides of the unit which may be positioned so as to shape the beam for your purposes. You may want light on the wall but not on the ceiling, so you rotate the bar doors until one is at the top of the lamp housing, and then, just as though you were pulling down the brim of a cowboy hat, you can shade the light down on the wall where you want it. Barn doors are also useful when light from a unit is spilling onto a foreground object and washing it out. By feathering the edge of the light with the flap, the intensity on the foreground can be reduced so as not to be obtrusive.

Every manufacturer of lighting units makes various devices for modifying the light beams thrown. For diffusion of the light, stainless steel screens are often used. For intensification of the beam, a reflector skirt may be used. Holders for color filters can be snapped onto the front of the unit. Of great importance when using lights for outdoor shooting are the new dichroic filters, which convert the color of the light beam to match that of sunlight. These are much smaller and much more efficient than the filters formerly used for this purpose (see discussion of color matching in Chapter 5).

One device often used to shape a light beam is called a gobo. This consists of a piece of thin, opaque material such as Masonite, cut into a pattern and held in the light beam so as to cast a shadow pattern. It is frequently used to liven up an otherwise very plain background. You can sometimes see the result in a TV commercial where the product is in the foreground and the background consists of an irregular light pattern.

It should be concluded from this chapter that lighting for films is a matter of thinking what you want something to look like and then putting light where it will be reflected to give the desired image quality. Bringing up the level of illumination to the point where it yields sufficient exposure is really only secondary. If we had a film stock so supersensitive that no additional illumination were necessary, the film cameraman would still continue to evaluate his scenes very much as I have outlined and would still use lighting units to help make his images special.

Every film-maker has his own personal style of lighting. Fads in lighting drift in and out. Sometimes extremely diffused lighting is favored, as in many commercials in color television. Sometimes very contrasty lighting is used for high-powered dramatic effect. Currently there are many films in which most of the facial area is lit with diffused fill light, and the main light is so far off to one side that it becomes a semi-rim light. This is a particularly attractive effect in color because it yields very rich, glowing skin tones; yet it has a lot of contour punch because of the bright semi-rim light. But whatever the style, the purpose is always the same. The film-maker is a craftsman in images, and he uses whatever lighting is necessary to make his images effective.

5

film stock emulsions

A length of motion-picture film consists primarily of a base, with perforations along the edge, and a photosensitive coating on one side of the base called an emulsion. There is a fairly wide variety of types of emulsion, each with characteristics that yield different kinds of images.

If you intend to shoot 35mm color, the most often used stock is Eastman color negative, type 5254. This film has an exposure index (ASA) of 100 when used with tungsten light, and an index of 64 when used in daylight with a conversion filter. The reason for the use of conversion filters is based on the fact that there is quite a difference between the color of white light from a tungsten source and the color of white light from daylight. In everyday life we make psychological adjustments for this difference and thus are not apt to notice it. But when we see shots made under the two types of light spliced side by side in a movie the difference is disturbingly evident—the sunlit scenes will have a bluish overcast and the tungsten-lit scenes will have a yellow overcast. This difference in the color of what is apparently white light is expressed in Kelvin degrees, or, in popular jargon, color temperature. Eastman color negative is designed to be used with tungsten light of a temperature of 3200 K, which is the color temperature of most lighting units discussed in Chapter 4.

With light of this temperature, it will yield a color image that looks natural. If you shoot scenes in daylight illumination, however, they will have a bluish tint, unless you use a *conversion* filter that is slightly salmon-colored. With this filter, the color of scenes shot in daylight will look natural, but since some of the light is blocked by the filter, the effective exposure index of the film is reduced to 64. The reason for making a color-balanced film stock for tungsten light, and not making one for daylight, is that it is much simpler to take the conversion filter in and out of the camera to handle both kinds of light than it is to unload and change the film every time you change the light conditions. For the Eastman family of color stocks the standard conversion filter is a Kodak Wratten #85. These are available either in glass or in gelatin squares, and may be mounted either in front of the lens or in a filter slot in the body of the camera, depending on what particular hardware you are using.

Since we will be referring to different types of film stock throughout this book, it is important to understand the meanings of the terms "negative film," "reversal film," and "print stock." Negative film yields an image of negative polarities: When it is printed onto print stock, the polarities are reversed, and a positive image is obtained. Reversal film yields an image of positive polarity, and when a print of it is made, it is made on reversal film so that the image will stay positive. Print stock reverses the polarity of whatever type of film is printed onto it.

In many industrial applications, duplicate prints made from the camera original are not desired; the original is projected directly, as is the case with home movies. A good choice of 35mm color stock in this case would be one of the Ansco-chrome reversal stocks made by GAF, in ratings of 100, 200, and 500.

For general-purpose shooting, the main reasons for using a negative color stock are lower overall costs, if a number of duplicate prints are desired, and much more latitude in exposure variations (see Chapter 6).

Black-and-white films in 35mm are all of the negative type. Eastman XT, type 5220, is rated at 25, and in return for this low "speed" gives images with very little "grain" pattern visible. A general principal in film emulsions is that as the exposure index increases, so also does the graininess of the image, and so the very high indexes are ordinarily used only when there is no other way of getting acceptable exposures.

For general-purpose black-and-white shooting, there are two good choices of stock. Dupont "Superior" 2, type 936, is often used, and is rated at 125. A comparable film is Eastman Plus-X, type 4231, rated at 80.

In the higher-speed indexes, Eastman makes Double-X, type 5222, rated at 250, which is remarkably fine-grained for a film of this sensitivity. Dupont "Superior" 4 is rated at 320, and Eastman 4-X, type 5224, is rated at 500. The latter two film stocks should be used with the understanding that they will yield images which, in comparison to the general-purpose stocks, show more grain pattern and less rich blacks.

In 16mm color, negative stocks are rarely used, except for TV news. Because of the smaller frame size, grain patterns assume even larger proportions. Since reversal stocks are somewhat finer-grained than negatives, and since they do not show scratches and dust so readily, they have become the standard in 16mm color shooting. Eastman Ektachrome Commercial type 7255 is the general-purpose stock most often used, and is rated at 25 for tungsten and 16 for daylight with a conversion filter. If you project this stock you will see an image of subnormal contrast and very pastel-looking colors tending toward the warm end of the spectrum. This distortion of naturalness is deliberate and is based on the fact that when duplicate prints of this film are made, the contrast and color shifts unavoidable in the duplicating process shift these factors into correct balance in the resulting print. By comparison, Kodachrome II, an excellent stock, but rarely used professionally, yields balanced color and contrast directly in the camera original, but when duplicated gives prints of second-rate quality.

For shooting color reversal under limited light, Eastman Ektachrome EF can be used at its ratings of ASA 125 for tungsten and 160 for daylight.

16mm black-and-white negative films are available in the same emulsions as listed for 35mm. In addition there are three black-and-white reversal stocks, Plus-X, rated at 50, Tri-X, rated at 200, and 4-X, rated at 400. Plus-X and Tri-X yield images of very fine grain and with deep rich black tones. 4-X shows a moderate grain pattern and blacks not quite so dense. In comparison, prints made from the negative versions of these three emulsions show mild grain and softer contrast.

In deciding whether to use negative or reversal in 16mm the following points may be helpful. Under conditions where light levels cannot be controlled and exposures may vary quickly (most often encountered in documentary and news filming), negative material is more forgiving and more likely to yield acceptable prints from incorrect exposures. When the processed negative is handled in editing procedures, the slightest speck of dust or the faintest fingerprint or minutest scratch will show up in the print made from that negative as a white blemish, whereas the same imperfections on a reversal original will print as black blemishes, which are far less annoying. The visible grain pattern in a print made from a negative is more noticeable than that of a print made from a reversal material. The total cost of stock, developing and making a print from negative is about 18 per cent less expensive than doing the same thing with reversal. The graphic image quality of prints made from reversal is somewhat richer and more sumptuous-looking.

The choices of stock in 8mm and Super 8 are presently quite limited. Kodachrome II in either 8mm or Super 8 is as good a color reversal stock as there is. Duplicate prints may be made at a few laboratories, but do not expect very good quality. If good-quality prints are necessary in 8mm or Super 8, it is best to do the original shooting in 16mm and then make 8mm reduction prints. If duplicate prints are not necessary, then doing the original filming in an 8mm gauge is by far the most economical procedure.

If you use the Fujica camera mentioned earlier, the only stock available is Fujichrome Single 8 (a Super 8 format). This is rated at 50 for the tungsten type or 25 for the daylight type. Since this comes in a quick-change cartridge, it is easy to switch back and forth between the two types for tungsten or daylight shooting. The color and sharpness are very similar to Kodachrome II.

Black-and-white film is available in limited quantities in 8mm and Super 8. The two best choices are Plus-X and Tri-X.

In addition to the film stocks described so far in this chapter, there are some special-purpose emulsions available in 16mm and 35mm. Dupont makes a Rapid Reversal Pan, type 930, which is designed for very quick processing. The film can be completely developed to a reversal image and then dried in a total time of about 11 minutes. This film is rated at 80 and is also available at a rating of 200.

For special effects it is sometimes desired to have an extra-high contrast in a black-and-white stock. This characteristic is also useful for making objects seem to stand out very clearly against their background when both are of about the same brightness. Dupont makes a negative stock, type 140, for this purpose, and rates it nominally at about 200, cautioning that exposure is difficult to calculate and that testing of a roll under the conditions anticipated is recommended. Another way of getting high contrast in black-and-white is to shoot on regular negative and make a print on high-contrast print stock. Such a stock is made by Eastman, and if you plan to use it for printing, consult the printing lab. High-contrast negatives and positives are made in both 16mm and 35mm.

Film stock which is sensitive to infrared radiation rather than to visible light is available from Eastman in both 35mm and 16mm. The creative uses of such film have hardly been explored at all, although technical applications are quite common. Outdoor scenes come out looking very strange, with brilliant white foliage, very black skies, and black bodies of water. Scenes in which there is a great deal of visible haze come out crisp and clear to the farthest detail. Shots of faces show a pale skin, with lips almost as light, and eyeballs that are almost completely black. Using this film, it is also possible to illuminate a dark room with invisible infrared radiation and still be able to photograph. Its exposure index is about 80 for daylight and 200 for tungsten. If you want to use this stock be sure to consult a copy of Kodak's data pamphlet, "Infrared and Ultraviolet Photography" ($1.00), since there are some special procedures involved in using this material.

6

exposure control

A correct exposure is one that looks good to you. In determining what exposure level to use in a shot, the use of a meter which measures the amount of light is essential. But the meter does not know what your intentions are for the photographic appearance of the shot. It is capable only of measuring the amount of light available for exposure, and the lens settings that you use depend on what tonal effects you want.

Here is a good example of the subjectivity of exposure. The shot is of a person at the edge of the water. The sun is coming from behind the person, more or less, so there is a bright sunny sparkle on the water. The film is color, rated at 25, and the camera-running speed is 24 fps, yielding an effective shutter speed of 1/80 of a second. The question now is what T stop to set the lens diaphragm at.

(T stops are measures of the *actual* amount of light passed by the lens at different exposure settings. T stops are gradually replacing the traditional F stops, which were based on *calculating* how much light the lens would pass. The T stop numbers are a standardized series that run: T 1.4, T 2, T 2.8, T 4, T 5.6, T 8, T 11, T 16, and T 22. Not all lenses have the capability of this wide a range of T stops, but all lenses are marked with numbers from this series, whether they are calibrated in T stops or in F stops. The amount of light transmitted by a particular T stop is twice that of the T stop number to the right, and half that of the T stop number to the left. Thus, if we were shooting at T 4, and needed to pass twice as much light onto the film, we would open up to T 2.8. If we then needed to double the amount of light once more, we would open up to T 2, and so forth.) Suppose we take one frame at T 22, the smallest stop on the lens, then another frame at T 16, and so on down the line to T 1.4, in which case the lens is wide open. We now have nine frames, each exposed to twice the amount of the previous one, and somewhere between the two extremes we might expect to find the correctly exposed frame. But when we examine the developed strip of film, there are at least three good-looking frames out of the nine; thus there were three "correct" exposure settings for the shot. This is possible because there are two major areas of interest in the shot, the figure and the background, and each has a very different degree of brightness from the other. The frame exposed at T 11 is a very good-looking silhouette of the figure against a background of the water. The frame exposed at T 8 is a compromise for both areas and looks like an everyday pretty picture. The frame exposed at T 5.6 shows good detail in the figure, even though its surfaces are in shadow, and the water loses pictorial importance and merely suggests bright sun and water as a background. Which of the three pictorial effects described you want for your film depends on your personal preference and how the shot is to fit in with the rest of the film. By using an exposure meter in a knowledgeable way, any of these three tonal effects could be obtained at will.

An exposure meter is a fairly sim-

Exposing for good water detail results in a silhouette of the figure.

A compromise exposure halfway between. (Reflected fill light on the figure would bring figure and background brightness levels within the range of the film stock.)

Exposing for skin tone of the face washes out background.

ple device that responds to the amount of light present in terms of how far up a numerical scale its pointer moves. The calculator dial on the meter is then set to the pointer's indication, and a T stop and shutter-speed combination yielding the "correct" exposure is then indicated by the dial. The important thing to note here is that the meter is responding to the *light present*, not to a subject. It does not know if your subject is a white snowman in *dim* light, or a dark scarecrow in *bright* light. If you take a reading of either of them with a type of meter that measures light *reflected* by the subject, they both might read the same. (The other type of meter measures light falling on the subject, and is called an *incident* light meter.) *The reflected light meter will give you a reading which will reproduce the predominant area of the scene as a middle tone, halfway between black and white.* This is a very satisfactory method for the majority of photographic situations.

But what do you do when you want a predominant area of the picture to come out white, such as a snowbank, or black, such as a title background? Here is the method: You take a reading of the snowbank (which would reproduce it as a middle tone) and then deliberately increase the exposure over what the meter indicated. Increasing the exposure two stops (in reversal color) would render the snow white. In the case of the black background for the titles, you would again take a reading of the subject, but in this case you would reduce the exposure by about three stops to render the background as black. Exactly how much to shift the actual lens setting open or closed is a matter of experience with the particular film stock and laboratory processing you are using. The general rule of thumb is that if you start with a middle-tone subject (such as a tan face) you can render it photographically as white by overexposing it two stops, and black by underexposing it three stops. Lest this seem arbitrary to the reader and cause him to look for a meter that will give him a correct exposure reading directly, it must be repeated that all any type of meter can do is measure the light present, and that it has no way of knowing what it is pointed at or how you want your subject to be photographically reproduced. Since the majority of subjects a meter is likely to be pointed at will look properly exposed if they are reproduced as a middle tone, the meters are calibrated to indicate that automatically—and if you want some other tonal effect, you use that reading as a reference point and make alterations according to your desires.

Let's use this technique on the scene of the figure by the water. If a middle-tone exposure of the figure is desired, the meter reading should be taken of the figure *only*. Bring the meter right up close to the figure, where all it will measure is the brightness of its surface. Setting the lens based on this exposure reading will automatically render the figure as a middle tone. (If you were using a camera with an automatic metering system built in, you would then manually lock the lens setting to the T stop indicated by the closeup reading.) You then move back to the previous camera position and make the shot. The reason you cannot make the exposure reading from the camera-shooting position is that from there the meter would include, as about half of the area it saw, the very bright light from the water, and would give a setting that would not render the figure as a middle tone.

Now, suppose you wanted to reproduce the foreground figure as a silhouette against the water. You would then take a meter reading of the figure only and deliberately set the lens for three stops less exposure than indicated for a middle tone.

If you deem the figure and the water background equally important, then you would take a meter reading from the camera position, which would average the two areas of brightness to give you a compromise exposure. The figure would then be about one T stop darker than middle tone, and the water about one stop lighter.

To sum up, when you want a particular area of illumination in the frame to appear as a particular tone of light or dark, you take a meter reading of *that area only*, knowing that this reading will render the area as a middle tone, and then open up or close down the lens opening according to how much lighter or darker you wish it to appear.

In studio work where large numbers of lighting units must be set to predetermined levels, the incident type of light meter is most commonly used. The incident light meter is put where the subject will be and aimed at the camera position. The meter thus is measuring the amount of light *falling on* the subject (not reflected from it), and as the subject is darker or lighter, it will reflect less or more light and be rendered properly on film. For work under a wide variety of non-studio applications, the reflected light meter is more versatile than the incident type, and is the type built into both amateur and professional cameras.

In Chapter 4 a situation was mentioned in which a person is seen in what is purportedly the dark; but it is desired that a change in expression be visible in the face. Careful use of a meter will enable you to make such shots with no special difficulty. First you set the rim lighting up on the figure to a level where it will reproduce as a middle tone. This can be done by going right up close to the actor and measuring the light intensity on the side of his face toward the rim lights. Then take the T stop indicated and set the lens to that. Let us assume the meter said T 5.6. The next thing to set is the fill light for the face so that the expressions can be seen. This light should be diffused by some sort of scrim so that it will be very soft-looking, but this is not absolutely necessary. What is critical is getting just the right amount of underexposure on the front of the face. Four stops under would be quite black, three stops under very nearly black, and two stops underexposure would be just about right. Since we have already established our lens opening at T 5.6, what we need is an amount of light full on the face which gives an indicated exposure on the meter of T 2.8. Thus, since we are shooting at T 5.6, we are underexposing two stops. The edge-lit area of the figure is normally exposed and the full-face area is deliberately two stops underexposed. The effect of the shot will be, however, just what we wanted.

A favorite lighting scheme in professional films being shot in sunlight is to stage the action so that for the most part the sun is to one side of or behind the actors, functioning as a rim or contour light. Then the shadow areas of the actors' faces are filled in with enough artificial light to render them pleasantly visible.

Here is why all the effort of using fill light is worth it in an extended *sequence* of shots—say, where two people at the beach are talking. If we start the sequence with an establishing long shot of the couple, we would have to expose for the overall light value of the scene, since, in the establishing shot, their physical surroundings are more important than they are. Then, as the dialogue progresses, the audience gets more and more interested in what they are saying and how each is reacting to the other. Therefore the camera would be moved in for much closer shots of the couple, but since the faces are in their own shadows we cannot see them well enough. Opening up the lens a couple of stops solves that, but now the contour lighting from the sun is too bright and so is the ocean or sky area behind the couple. Then, as the man stands up, we cut to a shot from farther back and must change the exposure again. If this sequence were edited into the form seen by the audience, the background and the contour-light illuminations would be going up and down at almost every other change of shot, and this would certainly spoil the whole dramatic effect the actors and director worked so hard for. The solution for the film maker is to use just enough fill light on the faces and figures so that they are readily visible and attractive, and at an exposure setting that is compatible with that required by the background and contour lighting. Thus a balance between the levels of illumination in the scene can be set up, and a constant T stop used throughout the various shots of the sequence. This is one of the cases we will encounter in this book in which motion-picture photography varies from still photography, due to the fact that movies are perceived as a continuum, rather than as separate shots. A realistic-looking balance between the faces and backgrounds could be gotten by basing the exposure on the background and illuminating the faces to one stop less exposure than that. In this way the sense of sunshine in the background and the sense of shade in the foreground would not be spoiled by the artificial overtheatrical appearance that would be obtained if we balanced faces and background to the same level of illumination.

In some situations there is no reasonable way of making an exposure measurement. Such a case would be a pattern made of pinholes punched in a piece of metal, with the illumination coming through the pinholes. Fortunately, exposure setting on this kind of subject is not very critical. If the shot is fairly brief, and is easily repeatable, then the cost of shooting it three times at three different trial-exposure settings is negligible compared to the assurance of getting a good take. This is a very good way of handling such things as sunsets, cities at dawn and at dusk, shots of the sun itself, and certainly wherever a variety of exposures would yield a variety of usable effects.

In cases where no accurate readings can be taken, and where, in addition, the shots involve a lot of action that would be disastrous and costly to restage, and are of such length that it would cost too much to run the scene at several exposures, there is a commonly used technique which will usually give good results. Shoot a short test roll of the area in which the action is to be staged, or of the unusual subject matter, and try every possible exposure you think might have any value. Projecting this and seeing what works out before you do extensive and expensive shooting will let you determine just how the scene should be photographed.

7

looking at action

Among the many reasons for film's being an interesting medium is its ability to be an ideal viewer. The camera's vantage point can always be the best place to see any part of a series of actions. If we compare a film of some actions in a baseball game to what a person in the stands could see of those same actions, the difference in vision is quite startling. The pitcher takes hold of the ball. The camera shot of this is a big close-up showing that he is holding it in such a way as to throw a curve ball. He winds up. This shot shows him in full figure, so we can see the details of the lifting of his knee for balance and the twisting of his shoulders as he gets ready to unleash the ball. The batter tenses his grip on the bat, and his eyes narrow in anticipation. This shot is medium-close, and perhaps the camera has now turned around from looking at the pitcher and is shooting in the opposite direction, toward the crowd. In the next shot the pitcher throws the ball, with a very hard snap of his arm. The flight of the ball is the next factor of interest, and it would be well to pick a camera angle that shows whether or not the ball really did curve after all. This could be done by shooting from the pitcher's viewpoint, and since the ball would be receding directly away from the lens, any curving in its path would show clearly. The disadvantage of this viewpoint, however, would be that the ball would also appear to be getting smaller, and the batter, who is now more important than the pitcher, would be a small figure in the background, while the pitcher would be a large figure in the foreground. Putting the camera where it could see the ball coming head on would be a better solution. We could see that the ball does curve; we see it approach the plate; the bat swings into the ball and knocks it high into the air. The next shot shows an outfielder looking up and shading his eyes from the sun with his glove. In the meantime the batter is running for first base. We switch back to the fielder, who is just reaching to catch the ball. As he does, the sun gets in his eyes, and he misses the catch. This last sentence of description needs at least three shots to show clearly all that happened, just as the sentence itself is divided into three parts by the commas. The fielder starts to reach out his glove for the ball. This is shot from his side so that the extension of his glove hand, although very slight, is easily noticed. To show that this allows the sun to get in his eyes, we need a closeup of his face with the shadow of the glove moving away from his eyes. We then could use a shot looking over his shoulder up into the air with his glove at first blocking out the sun—then, as the glove moves, the sun would shine directly into the camera lens, creating a dazzle. Then we could use a shot of the ball plopping to the ground next to his feet. His hand reaches into the camera frame of view and grabs the ball. The next shot is from the stands; it shows him throwing the ball to second base just as the runner is making a dash for it.

The series of shots that could be made to show whether or not the runner made it safely to second base would involve clear thinking about what aspects of the action are most important or most interesting, and then imagining these from various camera vantage points. Playing these imaginary shots quickly through your mind enables you to choose the ones which will show best what happened. The ability to do this well can only be developed through experience, but understanding the principle of the ideal viewer can make your experience much more rewarding. This principle is so basic to filmic design that it hardly matters what your subject is, or what style of film you are making. In a film that is acted out, there is time to think about what aspects of a larger field of action you want to show. You can even write them down and consider that a shooting script. In documentary work you don't know what is going to happen, so you have to look at things with extra perception and think very fast about what aspects of reality you want to film.

What we have done in the baseball sequence just described is to take what is purportedly a continuous line of action and break it up into component pieces, each of which we photographed from the vantage point and distance that best showed that particular part of the action. Later on, in the editing stage, we will take these pieces and reassemble them into an apparently continuous action. As the viewer sees the film, he will be seeing the game from the pitcher's point of view, then from the umpire's, then from the fielder's (and exactly why he missed the ball), and then from a fan's point of view in the stands—all in addition to possessing a magical ability to be instantly at just the right place to see each detail of the action as it unfolds. There probably is no principle of the craft of film-making more important than this fragmenting of reality for later reassembly into a filmic form.

A variation of the kind of filmic designing we have been exploring is the insertion of visual details into a series of overall shots of activity. Suppose the scene is one in which there has been somebody badly hurt, and a woman phones for an ambulance. We could shoot the overall scenes on the basis of showing her making a phone call, talking, and then hanging up. Having completed this, we could go back and shoot details to be cut into the otherwise continuous scene of making the call. We first ask ourselves, What are we trying to show here in terms of feeling, as well as action? She's probably very upset, scared, in a hurry to get medical help. The otherwise ordinary act of dialing a number is suddenly very difficult. Her hand is shaking, her finger misses the right dial hole, and when she finally dials the number she is going to be impatient to have someone answer it quickly. How can we show this? Perhaps a shot of her biting her lip. When somebody does answer the phone, she is relieved and grateful. The telephone itself becomes a friend in crisis, and she holds it with both hands. These visual details can be inserted into the already shot overall actions during the editing of the film. They are of vital importance in expressing the woman's emotional state to the audience, and in inviting the audience's empathy.

In the previous example it really didn't matter whether this was a preplanned scene done by an actress or one that really happened just as described. In either case the filmic thinking is the same. The inserts might have been called for in the script if it were an acted film, or the director could have thought of them after the overall scenes had just been completed. If the scene really occurred and was covered by a documentary film-maker, he would have noticed those vital details and made a point of getting shots that showed them. But whatever the conditions were, somebody—whether scriptwriter, director, or cameraman—had to think of those detail shots.

Where the camera is in relation to action can make the difference between a shot expressing your intention and expressing just the opposite. In karate practice the kicks are not actually aimed at anyone; in filming such a scene, if your camera angle shows the kicks going into empty space, the viewer will get the impression of futility and lack of real physical threat in the person doing the kicking. On the other hand, if the camera is placed so that the kicks come toward the lens, the impression is one of attack and the viewer will tend to flinch, even if subconsciously. An extreme example of this relationship is the difference between the camera's being in the plane that is dropping bombs—thus seeing the explosions as pretty patterns on the ground far below—and its being next to a group of people on the ground who are blown apart by the bomb.

The term "camera angle" is most often used in reference to the graphic composition of a shot, but its real importance lies in how it shows what is happening. In documentary films showing squalid living conditions the cameraman often makes the serious mistake of framing and composing his shots according to his usual habit of making his photography look good, and as a result what he gets on the screen gives a far more pleasant and ordered impression than is true of the real environment. This example is not meant to suggest that the solution is to get sloppy. Instead, it points out that the film-maker's camera technique should be appropriate to the feeling he wants his images to give the viewer. The point of good cinematography is to make the audience see and feel, and whatever camera techniques will accomplish this are good techniques for the occasion.

One of the most important aspects of any motion is its direction. Learning to see motion in terms of its direction on the screen is a prime part of the film-maker's craft. A good subject is a playground set of children on swings. Looking at the swinging action from directly in front of a single swing, you will see the swing come toward you and then recede. But there is also a major up and down motion present. If you were to film this action with the camera held stationary, the swing, in relation to the borders of the frame, would be seen to move up and down on the screen, in addition to appearing to move forward and backward. This is not just an academic observation. It means a lot of things, because this shot in your film will be preceded by a shot and followed by another, thus creating a context of motions. For example, this shot could be intercut very smoothly with a see-saw which is also going up and down. Looking at the swing from the side shows an arc as the direction of motion, with the two ends of the arc higher than the middle. If you are going to intercut this with a girl dancing, then getting a shot of one of her movements making a similar arc will flow smoothly with your swing shot. You can get still another direction of swing motion by climbing up on the swing's framework and shooting down, with the camera held so that the direction of the swinging motion is from side to side. Or rotate the camera one quarter-turn, and the motion will sweep up and down the screen, giving a much more dynamic up and down than that of the first camera angle mentioned. The camera allows the film-maker to take great liberties with "reality." It should be apparent from the preceding examples that any single motion can be made to go in any screen direction you want, simply by your choice of camera position in relation to the action.

When the film-maker wants to present a person or happening by degrees, rather than all at once, he can place his camera and frame the shot in such a way as to control what the audience will see, and just how quickly more will be revealed. For example, a couple is walking toward an apparently abandoned barn. Then, in a fairly close shot of an edge of the barn, we see a rifle barrel slowly poking around the corner. More and more of it comes into view, then the brim of a battered hat, a nose, and then a suspicious-looking face. Obviously a great deal of the interest of this scene is due to the controlled revealing of the person with the rifle. The simple act of training the camera on the edge of the barn so that the lens could not see all of the rifleman at once made all the difference in the effect of the shot. The results of this technique, widely used in theatrical films, rarely fail to appeal to the peek-a-boo instinct. For example, in those horror films where we get only glimpses of a scaly hand or an evil eye, the director accomplishes two purposes at once. Our curiosity is aroused to a high degree about what the monster looks like, and the revelation of the complete monster itself, on whose appearance so much effort was expended by the special-effects crew, is spread out in time throughout the film, and thus made to last much longer than if it had been effected right from the beginning.

One important kind of action in film is often overlooked by film makers. This involves persons or things coming into the frame of view or out of it. Let us imagine a scene where a man is making a militant speech to a cluster of excited people in front of him. He winds up his appeal by asking for a volunteer to parachute onto the Pentagon. Nobody answers. Then a man leaps up out of the crowd and says with great emotion that he will do it. Now, if you shoot this scene from a general overall viewpoint, you will miss the opportunity of playing on the audience's suspense as to whether anybody will volunter and, even more importantly, miss giving the audience a good visual surprise when some one does say he will do it. But, by setting the camera just above head level of the crowd, looking out over their faces, you could then have the person who is going to volunteer be standing right in front of the camera but with his head just outside its frame of view. The voice of the speaker asks for volunteers. Among the faces in the crowd we see no one responding. Will anybody? A face bobs up excitedly into the frame, almost filling it, and shouts Yes, he will do it. The visual act of the huge face popping up into view unexpectedly and filling the entire screen is a very strong happening and appropriate to the drama of the situation. The effect is achieved by thinking in terms of where the camera is placed and where its limits of the edge of the frame are. Selective framing is an extremely powerful filmic technique, applicable to a wide variety of film subjects. It is not used nearly as often as it should be. The film-maker should bear in mind that what is deliberately excluded from the frame of view is sometimes as important as what is included.

A peculiar and disconcerting thing often happens in closeup shots of action. On the screen they just happen too fast to be appreciated. For example, a man is shown getting on his motorcycle, and then there are big closeups of the key turning the ignition on, and his leg cranking down the kick starter. In real life, kicking the engine over is a special gesture in which there is a kind of physical satisfaction. As a result, the rider doesn't notice that the actual stopwatch time required is about a half second. This is only twelve frames of film at sound speed, and on the screen it is gone in a flash.

Another reason for the apparent speedup of action in large closeup is that the *screen* speed of a motion is increased in proportion to the enlargement caused by a small detail's being blown up to huge dimensions. The action of lighting a match, for example, when seen on the screen as a large closeup, is accelerated several times beyond its normal apparent speed as seen at arm's length.

This is one of many cases where action in a large closeup will look much better if you can stage it slower than it is normally performed. Television-commercial makers are well aware of this phenomenon and often use mild degrees of slow-motion photography to make visually satisfying the pouring of some liquid, or some granulated or cereal product (see Chapter 15 on special visual effects). A similar example is filming a girl brushing her long hair. One thinks of this in sensuous terms and expects that closeups showing texture and sheen would have this feeling. But the hand and brush will almost certainly seem, on the screen, to be jumping around much too fast and over-energetically, unless the girl brushes very slowly, or you shoot in slow motion.

Motion of an object is seen only in relation to other objects. This deceptively simple proposition is the basis for a great deal of creative accomplishment in films. For example, if an object is moving, but the camera is moving exactly with it, the object will not appear to move *on the screen* at all. The reason that we would perceive the object moving anyway is that its background would be moving across the screen in the opposite direction. A shot of the driver of a car, taken from the seat beside him, shows a stationary driver and car, but the background slides by in the direction opposite to the supposed direction of the car's movement. If there were no background seen out the window, then the shot would look the same whether the car was moving or not. What this means in principle is that we can control an audience's perceptions of motion by means of manipulating the relativity of the pictorial clues by which motion is perceived. Many spectacular examples are seen in the feature film *2001: A Space Odyssey*. A man is seen to fly toward the lens in a horizontal chamber of a space vehicle in which, because he is weightless, he may freely tumble about in midair. The illusion that he is weightless in a horizontal chamber is created by tilting the chamber set-up into a vertical position, putting the camera at the bottom looking straight up, and suspending the actor from a wire, on the end of which he may freely revolve. His own body blocks the view of the suspending wire. At another point in the same film, a stewardess is seen to walk up the side of a curved wall, and she continues until she is walking upside down on the ceiling. In actuality she remains vertical, and the whole foreground of the set, with the camera mounted firmly onto it, revolves in the opposite direction. Since the audience in the theater has no way of knowing which way is up or down (in real life the pull of gravity on our bodies tells us), it assumes that down is at the bottom of the screen, and since they see the whole foreground of the set remaining firmly oriented with the bottom of the room at the bottom of the screen, the only explanation for the stewardess' motion, *relative* to the borders of the screen and of the room, is that she is walking up the wall.

We, and a great deal of the world around us, are in motion all the time. Film-making is a craft that uses motion as one of its basic ingredients. Orchestrating motions into visual experiences of beauty and perception is one of the major things a film-maker can undertake. Understanding that all motions are parts of either larger or smaller motions is not easy. The movement of a crowd is made up of the movement of people, and the movement of people is made up of movements of parts of their bodies, and so on down to invisible atomic levels. Developing an ability to abstract from a sea of motions just those that will express intent is basic to film-making.

8

moving camera

We have simplified the analysis of motion so far by assuming that only the subject moves and that the camera remains stationary. Just as often, both the camera and its subject are in motion during a shot. The most basic reason for moving the camera is to keep a moving subject in the center of the field of view. Let's say we are filming surfers and that the camera is set up on a pier, giving a good view down the beach. In a wide-angle shot we see the complete scene, with the surfers picking up waves and riding them in (in some cases), and the people on the sand watching. No need to move the camera in this circumstance. But in order to get a closer view of the detail of one surfer and his board, you could switch over to a telephoto lens that could show him full frame, and as he picks up a wave and starts moving, you pan the camera to the left along with him as smoothly as possible. What you get on the screen then is an almost stationary surfer standing on his board while a lot of turbulent ocean slides rapidly past him. In other words, by the simple act of following him with the camera frame, you have reversed the fields of motion on the screen. A surfer who is riding toward your left becomes stationary in the middle of the screen, and the ocean roars by in the opposite direction, to screen right. As we have seen in the previous chapter, the screen motions of a shot become very important when you are editing the shot into a sequence, and you must become aware of screen motion if you are going to take advantage of it.

A professional approach to shooting the surfing scenes just mentioned includes using a good tripod and pan head. Although tripods are an extra piece of hardware to lug around and are at best clumsy and slow to set up, there are times when you've just got to use them. In this particular case, there is plenty of time to set the tripod up, and it will be a great help in getting really good shots. Professional tripods are heavy-duty devices, and they differ most from those used by still photographers in the design of the pan head on which the camera is bolted. This pan head, vital to the smoothness of camera motion, is usually made with large sliding surfaces that are greased. The amount of pressure on the pan handle required to rotate or tilt the camera can be adjusted by large knobs, which, if turned to their maximum, will lock the camera firmly in position. This type of pan head is commonly called a friction head, since it depends on varying degrees of friction between its sliding surfaces for smooth camera motions. Another type of pan head is called a fluid head, because moving the pan handle forces oil through an opening, the size of which can be adjusted for different rates of motion. This fluid or hydraulic resistance to moving the camera is very even, and it makes very smooth pans and tilts quite easy to accomplish. Going to all this trouble to achieve a supersmoothness in camera motion may seem compulsive until one realizes that whatever jerkiness and clumsiness appear in the pan of the surfer shows up on the screen as jerkiness and clumsiness *in the motion of the surfer.* Very probably, part of the meaning of the shot was how great it is to be in the middle of a crashing surf, riding on a little board with such skill and grace that you are truly a king of the waves. If the screen image of the surfer jiggles all over the screen in hesitant jerks, this meaning is entirely blown.

Many times you want to move the camera along with the action. There are a number of ways this can be done. Let us say the scene is part of a man's fearful fantasy that the photographer his wife works for is carrying her off for himself. This scene is staged in a huge cemetery with clusters of tombstones about as high as a man. The photographer is dressed in white satin, and in his arms he carries the helpless girl. Running after him in slow motion is the husband, arms reaching forward, but seeming to make little progress in catching up. By having the camera move along with the photographer we give the viewer a different feeling than if the camera stood back and merely panned to follow them. For one thing the composition of the shot can be set up to show the girl's head and hair hanging limply in a lower corner of the frame, while the photographer's evil face presses forward with confident power at the upper half of the frame. Being able to show these things clearly is more important than showing the physical progress of the trio through the cemetery, and therefore a tracking shot is much more appropriate to the meaning of the sequence than a panning shot. Since this sequence is to be construed as a fantasy, it will not do to have the audience feel they are

Pro-Jr. fluid head tripod.

looking *at* the action; instead, by tracking the camera, they will be more likely to feel they are being carried along *in* the action.

An even more subtle use of a tracking camera can be made in shooting the pursuing husband. In contrast to the confidence shown in the face of the photographer, we see here extreme consternation, a dream-like sense of frustration, an inability to move up, catch the evil one and get his wife back. If we track him from the side he will be seen to make pretty good progress against his background of tombstones. But if we roll the camera forward a little faster than he is going we will be leaving him slowly behind, which is exactly the feeling we want the audience to have. Also, if we pan the camera to keep him in frame as we pass him, the geometry of the shot is such that the tombstones he is passing as he runs will seem to remain almost stationary, further emphasizing his difficulty in catching up. (See diagram.)

Making smooth tracking shots can of course be done by setting up special rails on which there runs a little rubber-tired vehicle supporting the camera and perhaps a cameraman and assistant also. This is so costly and time-consuming that it is done only when absolutely necessary. There are special camera dollies made for studio use that roll smoothly as long as the floor is smooth. Aside from these solutions, there are some improvisational ways of making good tracking shots which cost little or nothing. A favorite technique of French directors is to use a wheelchair for the camera dolly and have the cameraman sit in the chair and hand-hold the camera. A wheelchair is very good for a number of reasons, the first of which is

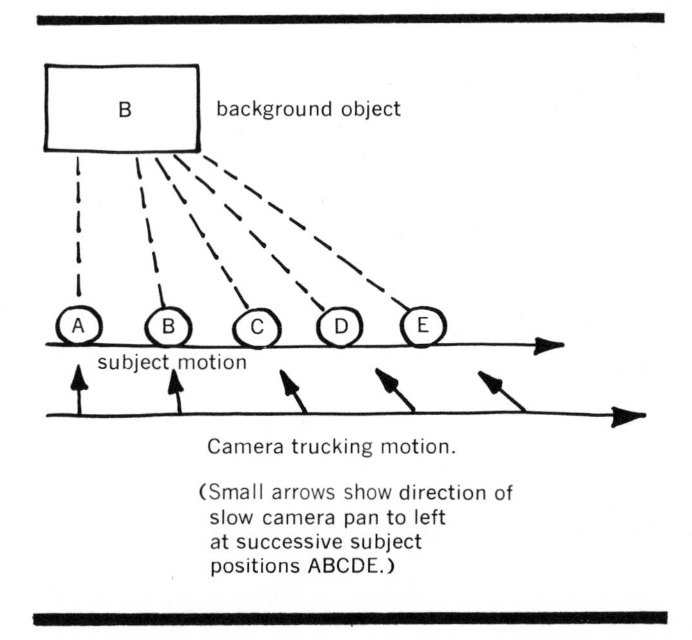

Camera trucking motion.

(Small arrows show direction of slow camera pan to left at successive subject positions ABCDE.)

its ability to turn on a dime. It is also very light, is designed to be pushed, and in many cases is even collapsible, so that it can fit into the trunk of a car. It has very large rear wheels (where all the weight is) that roll easily over cracks and small dips. Having the cameraman hand-hold the camera rather than mount it firmly on the frame of the wheelchair makes for a smoother motion, because the man's body acts as a natural shock absorber, thus insulating the camera from sharp vibrations. Another handy camera dolly is the kind of plywood plank with little rollers on it that mechanics use to slip underneath cars with. The cameraman can lie on his back and scoot along, getting a very low angle of view for special purposes, or he can lie on it on his belly and shoot straight ahead getting a cat's-eye view of the floor. Almost anything with wheels can be pressed into service. The main secret is having the cameramen hand-hold the camera.

The whole professional attitude toward hand-holding the camera has changed radically. The tradition was that it just was not done. But documentary and news cameraman often had to do so despite this tradition, and they discovered that holding a camera very steady could be learned, as one acquires an athletic skill. The design of the 16mm and 35mm Arriflex cameras included features making hand-holding quite satisfactory with certain lenses. In their quest for new ways of making the camera actively expressive, the independent, experimental, and advertising film-makers discovered that hand-holding the camera, and using the body as a camera mount, often gave visual results that were striking and useful, and that could not be gotten by any of the conventional means.

An interesting example of this

When in need of camera dolly, improvise. (photo courtesy Greg Prentiss)

technique would be in making shots for a film about the fun of riding a motorcycle. If you want closeups of the tailpipes and the rear wheel, the chain driving the sprocket, the road whizzing by, the rider's boot tip deftly shifting gears, his face as he zips up a slope through some trees, shots showing what he sees as he skims through a long puddle in the dirt road, then hand-holding the camera is by far the best way to get them. Trying to get such shots from a second camera vehicle is too difficult and too dangerous. Here are the factors to consider so that you will get good shots.

Trying to hold the camera steady by bracing it against your body, which is the usual technique when you are standing still, will be a disaster if you are moving on a bouncing vehicle. The secret is to hold the camera out at arm's length, where its weight tends to hold it steady, and as you bounce up and down, your extended arm acts as a pivot in relation to the camera and therefore does not effectively transmit your motion to it. This may sound strange, but it was discovered by trial and error to work quite well. Since you are unable to look through the camera viewfinder when shooting this way, you must rely on simply aiming the camera at the view you want. Since you are shooting things which are quite close, this is an accurate enough method under the circumstances. Another consideration is to use a wide-angle lens. This has two advantages, the first being that since this lens has a wide field of view at a short distance, it is that much easier to include what you want in the shot without looking through the viewfinder. The second advantage is that it greatly reduces the remaining jiggle to the point where the shots are acceptably steady (see Chapter 9 on lenses).

Some film-makers who have made a specialty of ski cinematography have, in order to get steady shots while skiing with the camera, taken the camera-at-arm's-length idea and extended it by means of a pair of aluminum tubes resting on the skier's shoulders, with the camera mounted about three feet in front of him on the ends of the bars, and a counterweight three feet behind him on the back ends. This idea could be applied to use in other rugged motion-shooting situations, perhaps horseback riding and running over rough terrain.

There is a shot in a feature film, *The President's Analyst*, which starts out as a closeup of the hero's face; then the camera starts to pull back and we see that he is standing on some sort of structure. As the camera continues to pull back it reveals that he is on the torch of the Statue of Liberty. What a wonderful camera platform the helicopter is! It approaches the ideal of a flying carpet that will support the camera eye anywhere and everywhere. The trouble with helicopters is that they vibrate a great deal. But there are very ingenious special camera mounts made for helicopters that work very well. These mounts can be used as camera stabilizers for shooting from almost any kind of camera vehicle. Prominent among them are the Tyler Helicopter System, and the F.&B./Ceco Aero-Vision Helicopter Mount. Rentals would be roughly $150 per day.

A moving-camera shot is particularly useful when it represents the subjective viewpoint of the person in the film. Fleeing from pursuers, the camera may charge through a field of high weeds. Falling from an airplane, the camera can become a skydiver. Or it can put on a face plate and go exploring under water. In the midst of a fight it is often called upon to take a few punches. In a waterproof plastic housing, it can be attached to the front of a surfboard and either look ahead, simulating the view of the surfer, or look back and see the surfer's footwork.

In a moving-camera shot the framing is constantly changing, so that selective framing, which was discussed in Chapter 7, can be obtained by moving the camera over a stationary field, thus enabling the film-maker to introduce picture information at a controlled rate. For example, in *Gone With the Wind,* we see a shot of a few nurses tending the wounded men laid out in a railroad yard. The camera begins slowly to pull back and lift up at the same time. As the frame of view widens and travels over the ground we see more wounded men, and still more, and when we think we have seen them all, the shot continues to pull back and up and show even more wounded men lying in the sun. The impression of the vast number of casualties is much more effectively communicated than if the shot had started out showing the whole field at once.

Another reason for moving the camera is to obtain close views of your subjects and still show their exact physical spacing in relation to each other. If you want to show a line of police blocking the entrance to a school, it is not quite as effective to build the sequence up out of stationary closeups as it is to backtrack in close along the line of faces. The same sort of reasoning would apply also to a sequence involving a chorus line or field hands picking strawberries, or an office filled with girls sitting at typewriters.

By far the most widely useful and

versatile camera mount for moving shots is your own body (provided you are using a liftable camera). When making panning shots, do so by pivoting your whole self, rather than just turning the camera. With a little practice you will find that pans can be made as smoothly by this method as with a good tripod (provided you are not using a telephoto lens). To move from one side of room to the other, take long sliding steps, and do not rest the camera against your head but hold it slightly away, and you will not jar it so much. Shots that call for the camera to be raised or lowered within the range of your height can be made as smoothly with your body as with a very elaborate crane. It takes a little practice and care, but it can be done well. Professional film-makers often cover a subject first with conventional shooting just to make sure they have usable footage; then they start playing with unusual and difficult shots for fun, in the expectation that some of them will not only work but will be especially good. Try playing with camera motion next time you are shooting; you may well discover something new.

9

lenses and perspective

Being able to use a variety of lenses in making a film is a tremendous aid in getting visually exciting footage. Since we will be looking into all sorts of lenses of other than normal focal length, we need to establish what is meant by "normal."

It might seem logical that a normal lens would be one that sees the same angle of view as our eyes. This angle of view is about 180°, or a half circle. But a camera lens with this field of view would be called a superwide angle lens. What is considered a normal lens in cinematography is one that is half the focal length of the projector's lens. The idea behind this is that no matter what focal length of lens you use to make a shot, if you use the same focal length to project it with, and stand next to the projector, from that distance it will appear to be in "normal" perspective. The audience, however, is not standing by the projector, but is on the average, midway between the projector and the screen; thus, using a projection lens of twice the focal length of the camera lens compensates for this and the perspective appears normal to the audience. Once we have established the focal length of the projector lens and the general viewing distance of the audience, then using lenses of different focal length on the camera will produce varying effects on the screen.

The focal length of a normal lens

in 35mm is 50 millimeters. In 16mm it is a 25mm lens, and in 8mm a 13mm lens is considered normal. Using these figures as a basis for comparison will make discussion of various lenses much more clear.

Let's see what can be done with telephoto lenses. If we use a lens of twice the focal length of the normal, we will get an image of the subject twice as big as that obtained with the normal lens. At the same time, we get an angle of view half as wide. In other words, since we have enlarged the objects in the viewed area to twice their size, we can get only half as many of them in the frame. If the camera is being hand-held, no matter how steadily, the visible jiggle of the image is also magnified to an amount twice as apparent. The more powerful the telephoto lens used, the more the image is magnified and the more any camera motion is magnified. This is why a tripod was recommended for the panning telephoto shot of the surfer in Chapter 8. The telephoto lens provided the means of getting a fairly close view from the stability of the pier, but it then imposed the necessity for a very steady mount so that the shot would not jiggle excessively.

When a lens is focused on a subject, not only will it be rendered sharp, but objects some distance in front of and some distance behind the subject will be in acceptable focus also. This zone of acceptably sharp focus is called the "depth of field" focus, and is an important factor in choosing which lenses to use. Other things being equal, the more powerful a telephoto you use, the shallower will be its depth of field. This means that if you are shooting a moving object whose distance from you is changing, you will need to follow focus during the shot to keep the subject within the depth of field. Using a reflex-type camera makes this much easier since you can see exactly what the state of focus is through the viewfinder. The shallow depth of field of the telephoto lens is very often used to advantage. Suppose you want a shot of a pretty girl. Instead of having the camera close to her and using a normal lens, you could move the camera back twice as far, come back in optically by using a telephoto lens of twice the focal length of a normal one; her face on the screen would then be the same size as if you had used the normal lens, but the background of trees would be greatly out of the depth of field focus and would appear as an impressionistic pattern of light and color. Her head, being in sharp focus, would appear to stand out more clearly against the out-of-focus background, and the total effect would be one of an increased presence, or realness. Or, suppose you have a couple walking through the woods, coming gradually closer to the camera. By using a telephoto, you can put whatever attractive foliage you want between the camera and the couple, and since this will be radically out of focus, it will provide a good-looking impressionistic pattern of leaf color and give a heightened sense of the couple's being in the woods.

Another use of the shallow depth of field of the telephoto lens is selective focus. If you arrange various parts of your subject matter so that they are scattered at different distances from the camera, you can start on the closest one, then, during the shot, smoothly change the focus, causing that subject to go out of focus and another part of the scene to come into focus. What had been

Shot with a normal focal length lens, the background is fairly sharp.

Shot with a telephoto lens, the background becomes impressionistic, producing a more three-dimensional effect.

Shot with a normal focal length lens.

Shot with a telephoto lens from three times farther away.

just a background color blur behind the first subject can focus into a child playing in the grass. This is another one of the many ways in which the film-maker can control the perceptions of the audience in a way that is interesting to them.

The next thing to look into is perspective, and how we can use the telephoto lens in handling it. Perspective is the apparent size of an object in relation to the apparent size of other objects at *different* distances. Thus, the image of a man holding a can of beer out toward the camera could be presented with the beer can exactly the same height as the man's head—but moving the camera closer and switching to a wide-angle lens, we could create the image so that the beer can was several times as large as the man's head. Changing the perspective cannot be accomplished without changing the relative distances between camera and parts of the subject. Contrary to some opinion, lenses of different focal length do not have different perspectives. If we shot the man and the extended can of beer with a telephoto, a normal, and a wide angle lens (without moving anything), the *relative* size of the can of beer and the man's head would be the same in all three shots. Now, let's see how perspective relates to use of a telephoto lens. We have a shot of a track star running directly toward the camera lens, starting from a distance of 100 yards. If we put the camera on the finish line, using a normal lens, the image size of the runner will start small and get larger as he gets closer, and when he hits the lens at the finish line, his image will have enlarged to where his belly button will fill the whole screen. Now suppose we put on the camera a telephoto lens of six times the normal focal length. We can then back the camera six times farther away from the starting line and still have the same-size image of the runner back at the start line as we had with the normal lens. In other words, although we've put the camera six times farther away from the runner, we have brought his image up to six times its height by the telephoto lens, so in terms of image size at the beginning of the shot, everything looks normal. Now the runner starts and comes toward the camera. This time, as he continues running, he doesn't appear to be getting any closer. It looks as though he's running hard but staying in the same place. We think that he is not getting any closer, because his image is not getting any bigger. His image is not getting appreciably bigger because even when he has run the entire hundred yards he will have covered only one sixth of the distance between the starting line and the camera position, which is 500 yards beyond the finish line. We got a new perspective by moving the camera from the finish line to a point 500 yards beyond it. Then we got a "normal" image size of the runner at the start line by using a telephoto lens, which, by enlarging him, made us think we were standing on the finish line. The key thing to remember is that increase or decrease of image size due to movement is a ratio of the distance of the movement to the distance of the camera from the start of that movement. By this reasoning, if we have a shot of a runner standing six feet away from the camera, and he comes one foot forward, we will get the small increase of image size as if he had started from 600 yards away and had come 100 yards closer.

Another use of the properties of the telephoto lens can be illustrated by the following example. A drunk wanders out onto a busy boulevard and is to appear in imminent danger of being run over. He eventually makes it across to the other side, but he apparently had a very narrow escape. If we could see the scene from directly overhead it would be obvious that the actor was skillfully threading his way between the lines of traffic and was really in very little danger. If this scene is shot from the sidewalk, however, it is much harder to see whether the drunk is directly in the path of an oncoming car or is slightly to one side of it. Now, by pulling the camera farther back from the side of the street, and by using a long telephoto, both the drunk and all the cars on the road will appear to be in the same plane of action. The visual clues that would tell us which car is closer to the camera and just where the man is in relation to the cars are canceled out by the combination of camera shooting angle and the use of the telephoto lens. The same thing will work on a wide variety of subjects, wherever you want ambiguity as to the fore-and-aft spatial relations of a scene. A film joke based on the use of this principle shows a man and woman running toward each other from opposite ends of a field, and just as they are expected to meet they seem to pop through each other and continue running on across the field in opposite directions. They really have not come within several feet of each other, but the side view through the telephoto successfully keeps this a secret so that the surprise works.

A wide-angle lens has a much greater depth of field than a normal or telephoto lens, and is often used

Shot with a telephoto, both figures appear to be at equal distances from the camera.

The figures actually miss each other by about four feet.

for that reason alone. This large depth of field means that action can often be filmed without any need for follow focusing during the shot. It also allows for a huge variety of image compositions. At a cocktail party, for example, you could make a shot at which, close up at one side of the screen, is the martini someone is holding, in the middle of the frame are some people laughing, and at the far side of the room someone has just arrived in an amazing dress. Since a wide-angle lens allows you to get very close to subjects and still have a somewhat overall view of them, unusual angles that would be impossible with other lenses can be achieved. For instance, to get a shot of a man getting on a horse, you could sit on the ground under the left stirrup and aim the camera upward as the boot slips into the stirrup, and as the man swings into the saddle, you could move the camera just slightly away from the horse's belly and the whole figure of the rider, culminating in his broad-brimmed hat, would be seen in the frame. With a longer focal-length lens this shot would be impossible without digging a hole in the ground to get far enough down to include the whole figure in the shot.

The effect of a wide-angle lens on motion coming toward or going away from the lens is just the reverse of the telephoto's effect. The wide-angle lens produces a smaller image of a given subject at a given distance than does a normal lens, and so, to fill a frame with the subject, you will find yourself shooting in quite close. At these short distances, any motion of the subject away from you or toward you will take up a relatively large percentage of the small distance between the camera and the subject, and therefore the motion will appear to be exaggerated. An example might be helpful here. Suppose you have decided on a subjective camera shot in a fist-fight sequence. The bad guy is to throw a punch directly at the camera lens and come within a couple of inches of it. If you frame your shot to include the bad guy's chest, arm and head, and if you use a normal lens, then you will have to be about six feet away. When he throws the punch his arm will extend about three feet, or *half* the distance to the lens. His fist will therefore double in apparent size, giving a fairly dynamic impression. If you use a full wide-angle lens, you will have to move in to about three feet from the man in order to get the same framing on the body as you had before. When he throws the punch his fist will cover *all* of the distance to the lens and will increase in apparent size to the point where it will fill the entire screen, and blot out the picture.

The relative size of foreground to background objects can be changed greatly by a combination of camera placement and choice of lens. Suppose we have a person in the foreground and a mountain in the background, and we have just filmed them with a normal lens. In this shot the foreground figure stands just the height of the full frame of picture. If we switch over to a wide-angle lens, the foreground figure will fill only about half the frame height. If we then move the camera closer to him (or him to it) so that he fills the whole frame height again, the net result of the shot will be that the mountain will appear only about half as high as it did in the normal-lens shot. By a combination of lens choice and camera placement we have reduced the apparent size of the mountain.

We could do just the opposite with a telephoto lens. By using one of three times normal focal length, we can enlarge the mountain to three times as high as it appears in the normal-lens shot. We keep the foreground figure the height of the frame by moving the camera away from the figure far enough so that it will fit in the frame height.

A zoom lens does not have a fixed focal length, but is infinitely adjustable to all focal lengths within its zoom range. This makes it especially useful in situations where the camera-to-subject distance must remain constant, since the zoom lens may be set at a focal length that gives whatever size field of view is desired. Changing the focal length of the zoom lens during shooting either shrinks the image size of objects in the shot or expands them, depending on which way the control lever is moved. This effect is perceived by the audience as moving farther away or closer to the subject, and thus the term zoom.

An interesting effect could be gotten with the combination of a zoom lens and a camera dolly motion. We could start out the shot with the lens set in wide-angle position, and as we slowly pull the camera back from the foreground figure (which would shrink him), at the same time we gradually zoom the lens into telephoto position (thus keeping the figure the same size). The net effect in the shot is that the mountain will mysteriously enlarge to several times its original apparent size, while the foreground figure looks on in amazement.

Use of a wide-angle lens reduces apparent camera jiggle by whatever

Action filmed with a telephoto lens.

Exactly the same action shot with a wide angle lens from much closer to the subject.

percentage shorter its focal length is than a normal lens. The principle is just the reverse of the magnification of jiggle by the telephoto lens. This is another reason for using a wide-angle lens in situations where camera shaking is unavoidable, such as the motorcycle sequence in Chapter 8, or when it is desirable to walk around with the camera while shooting. This is a favorite technique of documentary film-makers, and if they are shooting in 16mm (which is most likely), they are apt to forsake all but their 10mm wide-angle lenses for hours at a time.

A zoom lens can be considered as a variable focal-length lens, since it is more often used at a single setting during a shot than it is used for a zooming effect. The novelty of the zoom effect soon wears off and begins to annoy audiences, so it is recommended that zoom effects be saved for the points in your film where they will really be effective. Getting from a long shot to a close shot can be done instantly with a direct cut, and if instead, you elect to go into the close shot by means of a zoom, there should be a good reason for it.

There are many cases where the zoom lens may be used to simulate a camera-tracking shot, and of course this saves a lot of effect. This is possible when there is little or no depth to the field of view. Zooming toward a poster on a wall will look just like a tracking shot, since everything in the shot is on the same plane. Zooming through a deep three-dimensional field of view such as an orchard does not look like a tracking shot at all; the perspective does not change in a zoom shot, due to the fact the camera and subject positions remain the same. In a tracking shot through

Shot with a wide-angle lens, the background appears quite distant.

Using a telephoto lens brings the background up much closer, even though the camera has been pulled back from the model far enough to keep her image the same size as in the wide-angle shot.

the orchard the alignment of trees with trees behind them is constantly changing, and persons hiding behind nearby trees will become visible as the camera passes those trees.

Zoom lenses are useful, but they do have some drawbacks. Only the very best ones are as sharp as good-quality fixed-focal length lenses. Zoom lenses are rarely able to have maximum apertures of as much as T 2, whereas fixed-focal-length lenses are commonly made in ratings of T 1.4. Zoom lenses are quite large and heavy (in the 16mm and 35mm models) and in cases where inconspicuousness is important they are a handicap. In the 8mm cameras, zoom lenses are standard equipment at maximum apertures of T 2. These come in a variety of zoom ratios ranging from three to one to as high as six to one. In comparing zoom lens focal ranges, remember that they have meaning only as a percentage of the "normal" focal length. For example, a zoom lens for an 8mm camera that has a maximum focal length of 34mm is not going to give appreciably more of a telephoto effect than a lens of 30mm. But a minimum wider angle of view than a lens of 11mm, even though in both cases the absolute difference in millimeters is four.

Lenses for 35mm cameras are commonly available in ranges from about 14mm wide angle to 250mm telephoto. Since the normal lens in this gauge is considered to be 50mm, the 14mm lens will give you an angle of view about three and a half times as wide as normal. The 250mm telephoto will magnify a subject five times larger than normal. One of the best and most commonly used zoom lenses is made in a ten to one ratio of 250mm to 25mm. For special purposes there are both longer and shorter lenses made. An ultrawide-angle 9.8mm lens can give very bizarre effects. Closeup shots of people's faces will be apt to look grotesque, with bulging noses and receding chins and foreheads. Shooting downward at your own feet as they move will show legs apparently six feet long ending in tiny feet a long distance down. At the other extreme, telephotos are made as long as 800mm, and if you need longer, a Questar telescope can be used.

A first-class zoom lens for a 35mm camera costs about $1,500. They can be rented for about $40 a day. Fixed-focal-length lenses cost between $100 and $400 per lens, and can be rented for about $7 per day.

For 16mm cameras the range of lens choices is very similar to that for 35mm. There are a number of good zoom lenses available, one of the favorites being the 12mm to 120mm. The ultrawide-angle 5.7mm lens costs about $600 and may be rented for about $7.50 per day. Extremely long telephotos from 400mm on up can be obtained for a rental of around $10 per day.

One of the best values in lenses for 16mm cameras is the line of Switar lenses made for Bolex cameras. These range in length from 10mm to 75mm (the most commonly used range), and are of first-rate quality at relatively low prices—around $160 per lens. Rentals are about $3 per day.

With the recently made 8mm cameras the zoom lens is not interchangeable with other lenses, and your only special modification might be a closeup supplementary lens for shooting large closeups.

10

matching the action in cuts

In Chapter 7 we explored the process of breaking continuous physical reality up into photographic pieces, or shots, so as to obtain an ideal view of each part of the action. A major consideration in editing these pieces of film into an effective whole is the matching of the action that is occurring at the end of one shot with the continuation of that action at the start of the next shot.

Let us suppose we have two shots we want to join. The first is of a couple sitting on a couch talking. The man gets up (he can be seen only from the waist down) and walks out of frame to the left. The second shot is taken from farther away and shows him getting up from the couch and walking screen left to the fireplace to put a log on the fire. Since we have wisely shot an *overlap* of the action of his rising from the couch we can theoretically cut from the first shot to the second anywhere during the overlapping action and maintain a logical physical continuity. We could run the first shot up to the point where he has just walked offscreen to the left, and then cut to the second with him going to the left and putting a log on the fire. This will play well enough because of the simple continuity of the direction of motion on the screen to the left. But, as always, the question arises in the filmmaker's mind of what he is trying to express and what state of mind the audience is in. In the seemingly simple example proposed there are several factors to consider. If, as was suggested, we hold the first shot until he has moved out of frame to the left, we have a progression of dynamics of graphic image that starts with the man mostly stationary on the couch, then rising and filling about half the screen, and then this half of the screen moves rapidly offscreen to the left, leaving a stationary girl on the couch. Then, at the cut to the second shot, we have his figure in full shot moving left once more toward the fireplace. In terms of dynamics, or of rhythm of the images, we have created a clumsy sequence. Its changes are abrupt for no good reason. It is like dropping the ball and then picking it up again, rather than fielding it smoothly.

We could try another version in which the first shot is held until the man is soon going to get up, and then cut to the second shot in which he does. If we do this, however, right at the point of the cut the audience will be required to adjust to the graphics of the new shot, and at the same time to see him rise from the couch. This will work acceptably (if that is all you are interested in), but it imposes a psychological difficulty on the audience for no particular reason.

Probably the most effective way of joining these two scenes would be to carry the first shot until the man had begun his rise from the couch. As soon as his figure moves upward, the audience will want to pull back and see the entire action, as their attention has been caught by the start of his movement. His rising from the couch can be continued and completed in the second shot, and in this way there is a maximum of satisfactions both psychological and formal. The audience has had its attention aroused by the start of the motion, and the cut into the wider shot satisfies this need to get a better look at what has started to happen. The graphic dynamics will flow in a smooth manner, and the continuity of screen direction of the man's motion to the left will be maintained.

Controlling the direction of motion on the screen is very important in some sequences, notably in chases, fights and long treks. Suppose we have a shot of a man riding his horse toward screen right. Then a closeup profile of his face, shot from the opposite side. When these two shots are spliced together, the horse will be going screen right and the man going screen left. Various confusions will arise in the audience as to whether the face they see is somebody looking at the rider of the horse or whether it is the rider going back in the other direction for something he forgot. A similar confusion can arise in combat sequences, where it becomes difficult to tell who is the enemy and who the heroes, since both are seen shooting in both directions. Unless the film-maker has a purpose in mind, confusions ruin sequences that have been filmed with great effort, and they can completely undermine the audience's confidence in the film-maker's work; therefore care must be taken to keep the screen directions consistent with clarity.

In a sequence of a conversation between two people, it is a standard procedure to shoot closeups of each of the two people talking in which the back of the other person's shoulder is seen to one side in the foreground. Once you have established that one person is on the left half of the screen and the other is on

She starts out walking screen left.

Is this her sister coming to meet her? Or the same girl shot from the opposite side of the path?

Has she just seen her sister coming toward her? Just a simple directional mixup puts all these distracting questions into the audience's head.

the right, you can cut back and forth between the two over the shoulder closeups with great ease, since each person stays on his side of the screen area regardless of whether we see the front or the back of his head. If you then move the camera over to the opposite side of the pair, all shots from this side will have reversed the side of the screen that each of the characters had occupied, and great confusion and awkwardness will follow. It is possible that this could be used to great advantage in the appropriate dramatic context. For example, a one-sided conversation, in which one of the characters was figuratively talking to himself and didn't care what the other person said, could be deliberately shot from opposite sides, so that when he said something while on screen left, he would then pop over onto screen right and answer it. The other person would then always be seen as the back of a head only, which would be effective in making him faceless. As the shots cut back and forth between the two sides of the pair of characters, the audience would get a very strong feeling of the conversation apparently going back and forth between the two people, but only the one face would be seen, and it would do all the talking and would switch back and forth between the left and right sides of the screen.

The various shots that you want to edit into a film differ in vitality. As the shot begins there is often a lot of waste time while things get under way. Then the core of the action will be developed, or the height of the facial expression will occur, and the shot may continue in length but not in vitality. What it had to convey has been conveyed and the rest is just taking up time. Learning to recog-

In cutting back and forth between these over-the-shoulder shots of the couple talking, both the front and back of her head are always on the left side of the screen, and the same is true for him on the right side of the screen.

nize the points of vitality in a shot is of prime importance, because doing so enables you to edit a film that is all vitality and no deadwood. It is this extra richness which is a major attribute of a good film. One of the reasons people like to look at good films is that they are more ideal than life. The camera is able to see things from an ideal spatial viewpoint that can instantly switch from one place to another when desired, and the editing can instantly switch to an ideal *temporal* point when desired. The audience is always put where the action is, and the action is always highlights.

Let us try a practical example of film editing in order to get the feel of building a sequence out of the vital pieces of the shots. The story is this: An Indian hunter peers out from behind a rock and sees a deer. He fits an arrow to his bow, aims and lets the arrow fly. It misses the deer and sticks in a tree. The hunter quickly notches another arrow, the deer bolts out of sight; the hunter is so mad he shoots his arrow into the ground in anger. We will assume that all the pictorial pieces needed to tell this story have been well photographed, using the appropriate lenses, angles of view, exposures, lighting and camera motions. In putting together these pieces of moving picture it will be helpful to think as though we were the audience seeing the finished film.

In the first shot there is a large boulder. So? An Indian's face rises up cautiously from behind the boulder. Who is he? What is he looking at? Cut to the shot of the deer. Oh, he sees a deer. Is he going to catch it? Cut to shot of hunter notching an arrow calmly to the string of the bow. He is going to kill it. Is the deer aware of him? Cut to shot of deer.

(We have already seen this deer, so this shot can be very brief, just enough to show that the deer has not noticed the hunter.) No, the deer hasn't noticed him yet. How is the shooting of the arrow coming along? Cut to hunter pulling back the arrow. Is he going to have to shoot far? Is it a difficult shot? (So far we have never seen the hunter and the deer in the same shot, so we need to be told how far away the deer is.) Cut to over-the-shoulder shot of hunter in foreground, deer in background. When is he going to shoot? Cut to closeup of hunter's intent face sighting down arrow. Oh, as soon as he has taken careful aim. (The audience is now in a state of suspense, and this can be extended a little by a series of brief closeups of the fingers holding the bowstring back, the wicked-looking arrowhead poised before its flight, the vulnerable deer unaware of the threat, the twitching facial muscles of the hunter.) Is he ever going to shoot? This suspense is going on too long. Cut to the hunter letting the arrow fly. Will it hit the deer? (The instant the arrow is gone we care not the least about the hunter, but about the deer.) Cut to the arrow zinging into a tree an inch away from the deer. What will the deer do? Cut to the hunter notching another arrow. But we are impatient to see what the deer is doing! (Your urge to hurry is just what the hunter is feeling. That is why the shot of the deer's reaction has been delayed a second.) Cut to long shot of deer bolting away. The hunter was going to shoot another arrow—we wonder if he will have time. Cut to the hunter fumbling. Will the deer get away? Cut to the deer disappearing into the underbrush. How is the hunter going to react to the loss of the deer? Cut to hunter pulling back bowstring and shooting his arrow angrily into the ground.

Assembling your footage with this kind of anticipation of what the audience reactions and questions will be is a great help in determining what shot should cut to what shot at just what point. It helps one to overcome infatuation with certain shots that are particularly good-looking or extra difficult to get, and instead to use only what you need to communicate to the audience.

It is true that the deer-hunter sequence just described could have been presented as a single camera take of the overall action, without any cuts in it at all. The sequence would, however, have had only a small fraction of interest and power of the one we just edited out of the separate pieces of action. The audience would have tried to do its own editing, looking first at one part of the scene in the frame, then another, as the point of interest shifted in the action. But none of the things they looked at could be seen nearly so well as in our version where we had closeups of detail and changing camera viewpoints, each selected to give an especially good view of the action.

The editing of this sequence makes use of a structural design known as parallel cutting. This means that the two parallel lines of action (those of the hunter and those of the deer) are often presented alternately—first the hunter, then the deer, then back to the hunter, then back to the deer, and so forth. Since the deer and the hunter are available in many separate shots, the film-maker can control the timing of just what happens and when, to an extremely close degree. For example, when the arrow just misses the deer and hits the tree next to him instead, we could let that shot run on longer and show the deer bolting out of the field of view. Or, instead, we could cut back to the hunter having any number of reactions, and then cut back to the shot of the deer just as he is fleeing. The length of time between when the arrow misses and when the deer flees would be quite different in the two examples. The time relationships between the different parts of the whole story can be adjusted with great finesse to make the sequence as exciting as possible. In this little story, the photographic breaking up of the action into discrete components not only allows ideal visual vantage points for seeing the action, but, just as importantly, allows the timing and the order of presentation of the shots to be skillfully manipulated in the editing.

So far, matching the action in successive shots has been explored as a way of telling a story effectively in pictures. It can also be used with finesse as an element of interest in itself. This use is based on the mind's insistence on continuity. Just as the successive still photos or frames of a motion picture are perceived as continuous motion, so are successive frames perceived when there is a cut from one shot to the next. If we start with a man throwing a football and cut from that shot, just as he lets it go, to a shot of an airplane flying in the same direction, and end with a shot of a woman catching a loaf of Italian bread, there will be a remarkable continuity running through the sequence of three shots, even though all three are of different subjects. There are several factors that aid this wonderful illusion.

If the direction of screen motion is maintained in all three shots, then the logicality is enhanced to the point where we see the sequence as continuous. Had the airplane been flying in the opposite direction the spell would have been broken.

If the apparent rate of motion is the same in all three shots, then it helps the illusion that the moving object in all three shots is the same object. The airplane poses a special problem here because, although it is flying at several hundred miles an hour, it is so far away that it hardly appears to move with appropriate speed at all. But unlike the football and loaf of bread, it probably has no background referents to show us how fast it is passing, and this allows us to manipulate the shot with the camera. Let us suppose the airplane is flying to the right. We can make our shot of it while panning the camera to the left, thus causing the plane to move at any rate toward the right of the screen that we like, depending on how fast we pan the camera. Since there are no background referents to give away the fact that we are moving the camera rather than the plane, the illusion will be effective.

If the size of the moving objects in all three shots is the same, the sense of continuity is further heightened. Since the size of an object can be controlled by how far the camera is placed from it, and also by what focal length lens we use on the camera, matching the apparent size of different objects can usually be accomplished.

There can be further elements of continuity such as shape of the objects, or color of the objects, or even similar texture. All of these can aid the illusion of continuity, but the most effective are those of similar direction, similar size, and similar rate of speed. Being aware of these factors at work in the joining of actions from different shots is the foundation of being able to make them blend smoothly.

Maintaining a consistent screen direction for a moving subject in a series of adjacent shots is sometimes not desirable for reasons such as shooting convenience, photographic composition, direction of sunlight and story exposition. When it is desired to change the screen direction of an event that already has been firmly established as going in a particular direction, it is imperative to shoot a transitional or neutral direction shot. If we have established a parade going toward screen left, we can turn the parade around smoothly by using a head-on shot in which, since the parade is coming directly at the camera, there is no screen direction, and then cut to shots of the parade taken from the other side of the line of march, which would show it going toward screen right. Screen directions generated by objects coming directly toward the camera really radiate from the center of the screen, since, as the objects come closer, they appear larger and are thus expanding toward the outer edges of the screen. This means that no matter what screen direction is contained in the shot following, an element of directional continuity will be carried through. Another interesting way to change direction is from an overhead-camera viewpoint. If you are above a subject moving screen right, then you can twist the camera as it passes and finish the shot with camera upside down, causing the subject to then be moving screen left. Since you are shooting down from an overhead position, turning the camera upside down in this case does not turn the world upside down, since the subject from overhead has no up and down.

Matching the action has no iron-clad rules. Every cut from one shot to the next not only has factors of its own but is perceived by the audience in the context of the whole film, and thus the more unusual and individual the film is, the more responsible the film-maker is to his own mind and sensibilities, rather than to the conventions of a craft. The film-maker must be aware of what happens at the cut, both in formal and in expressionistic terms, so that he can solve whatever difficulties there are, and take advantage of what opportunities are there.

Another factor that is often important at the point of the cut is the position of the point of action on the screen from one shot to the next. Suppose you have a shot of a girl raising a glass of wine from the tabletop to her lips. This shot is taken from the side, showing her in profile. Suppose you also have the same action taken from a head-on shot. You decide that you want to cut from the first shot to the second at the point where she has the glass lifted six inches from the table. You cut the first shot at that frame, and then find the frame in the second (head-on) shot in which the glass in just six inches from the top of the table. You then join (splice) the two shots together, confidently expecting the action to match and carry over smoothly from the first shot to the second, based on your care in matching the physical reality of the position of the wine glass at the cut point. But the camera framing of the two shots is probably quite different, and so the *screen* position of the glass at the end of the first shot might be in the upper half of the frame, and the screen position of the glass at the start of the second shot in the lower half of the frame, although it was true that in both shots the glass is six inches above the tabletop. When this pair of shots is projected, the girl's motion of lifting the wineglass is going to be very distracting, because she will start to raise it (cut), then it will jump to a lower position on the screen and then continue up again. The solution is obvious, although it is not consistent with "reality." Cut to the second shot a few frames later, when the wineglass is at the same screen height as it was raised to in the first shot, and although six inches of the lifting action are missing, the effect will be much more natural. There are so many considerations when editing a film that it often happens that a seemingly sensible rationale simply does not work when applied to a particular cut. So you try another. Out of the multitude of possibilities, there is usually one that overrules the others; and when a particular reason for cutting something a certain way does not give a good result, then you know that there must be a more dominant reason within the material, waiting to be discovered.

There are two methods for splicing film: the *cement* splice, and the *tape* splice. Answering the question of which is the best way to splice picture film is not an easy matter. A quick explanation of the terms "work print" and "original negative" will help make things clear. In professional film-making, the film that is run through the camera is developed, and a copy, called a work print, is made of it. All the editing, timing, cutting, projecting, and recutting are done with this work print, which gets very beat up by the time the film is finished. The film material that was run through the camera, called the original negative (even though in reversal is not negative), has been stored safely in an air-conditioned vault all this time. When the editing and sound work are finished, the original negative is taken out of the vault by someone wearing gloves and, in a dust-free room, is cut to match exactly, scene for scene, the pattern of the work print. It is from this cut original that the ultimate sound prints are made that the audience sees.

Cement splices are made by first placing the tail end of the first shot into the splicer, emulsion (dull side) up as shown. The top piece of the splicer is then clamped down on this film to hold it in place. The left-hand platen is then pressed down, which will trim off the strip of film to the correct length. The whole right-hand

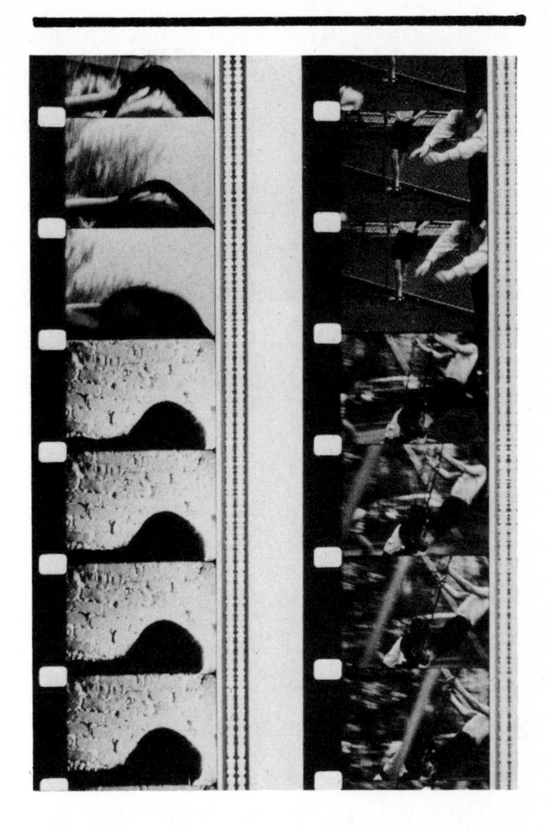

Two samples of match action cutting. On the left, the figure on the swing is carefully matched to the shape and motion of the girl lifting her head into the frame. On the right, the arms have just made a strong motion to screen left, which is continued in the next shot by the camera panning left with the figure on the swing.

In making a cement splice the cement is applied to the scraped portion of the film (center of picture), and the other scene in the right-hand clamp is then swung down on top of it.

splicer assembly is then lifted up out of the way. Then, place the head end of the next shot between the left-hand platen and clamp, and swing the right-hand assembly down to cut off the film to the correct length. A little area of film will be left exposed, the emulsion surface of which must be scraped off so that the cement will work properly. The cement is then applied to this scraped area, and *immediately* the right-hand assembly is brought down in place on top of it. After 5 to 10 seconds, the left and right clamps may be released, allowing the film to be lifted off the positioning pins of the splicer. That completes the splicing.

Tape splices are made by overlapping clear plastic tape onto several frames before and after the cut. The method for doing this depends so much on the design of the particular splicer used that the procedure cannot be summarized.

A cement splice made with a conventional splicer. Note the overlap both above and below the black frame line.

For editing the work print in any of the film sizes, either cement or tape splices may be used. However, if a cut spliced with tape is to be changed, the splice may be taken apart. A cement splice, on the other hand, is permanent, and the only way to change a cut is to cut the splice out, thus losing one frame of picture on each side of the splice line. For this reason, films containing sync dialog (where loss of these frames results in loss of sync) are most often spliced with tape. Since a frame is only one twenty-fourth of a second at sound speed, there are many types of films where this frame loss is of no consequence.

For splicing together the original camera material, preparatory to making prints for exhibition, the cement splicing method must be used, because although the splicing tape method uses clear tape, it causes an optical disturbance of the two or three frames on each side of the cut point where it is overlaid. The visibility of tape splices in the work print is of no concern because it is not the final product, meant for public exhibition.

In 16mm and the two 8mm gauges there is the additional problem that there is no blank space on the film between subsequent frames, and the slight overlap of the two pieces of film spliced together by the cement method will show fleetingly during projection. In 16mm there is an ingenious method of assembling the original material so that it may be printed without visible splices. This is called the "checkerboard" method and will be explained in Chapter 20.

If you are working in one of the 8mm gauges you are probably not going to be making prints, but will be projecting your reversal original instead. There is at present no way out of having your splices fleetingly visible. Either the cement method or the tape method may be used, although for mechanical reasons the tape splices work a little better in 8mm.

For splicing original material for printing, in both 16mm and 35mm, a special type of splicer called a hot splicer is used; this applies a little heat to the cemented area to dry it quicker and make the splice stronger. The 16mm version of the hot splicer also overlaps the film pieces in such a way that all of the overlap takes place on one side of the frame line only. This is necessary to the checkerboard method.

11

expanding and compressing time

Controlling the apparent rate of time flow in a film is one of the easiest things to accomplish and yet one of the most often overlooked by beginners. Let us try expanding a comedy sequence so that it will be more fun. Sitting at the edge of the swimming pool is a group of people sipping martinis. Unnoticed by them is a man going out to the end of the diving board, who, after a little preliminary bouncing up and down, takes off and does a tremendous "cannonball" into the water. The splash rains down upon the cocktail group, causing various reactions and refilling a few glasses. In "real" time this whole action would go very quickly, and the scene would hardly have time to produce much amusement for an audience. But expanding the time scale of the leap and the splash, will make the sequence vastly more entertaining.

First, we need an overall view to establish the situation. Then, a medium shot of the guy walking onto the diving board. Then, a fairly close view of the cocktail group, showing both what they look like and their unawareness of the jokester. Then, back to the man on the board, who by this time is just approaching the end of the board. He starts bouncing on it with little bounces that keep getting higher. To express this, we could use successively closer shots that would portray the action as actually getting larger on the screen. A very brief shot of the poolside group would be useful here as a reminder that they are still unaware of the diver, and as a way of connecting them, by association, with the bouncing on the board. We now need a series of shots that express the diver's determination to make a very large jump so as to make a very large splash. A wide-angle shot taken from below the board, looking up at the diver, could show him crouching upward into a leap. By shooting this upward motion and expansion into the air several times and from several angles, we will have enough footage to construct in the editing a "super" leap lasting several times as long as a single leap. Following our wide-angle shot looking up from below the board, we could use a head-on medium closeup of the man's determined face moving upscreen, then a side view of his legs springing up straight, then a closeup of his feet leaving the board and disappearing upscreen, then a shot that starts with a clear blue sky background with the diver's full figure zooming up from the frame line up toward the top, then a similar shot showing his legs and feet zooming upscreen and out of sight. By this time we have got him figuratively a long way up in air, so we need a shot in which he floats up into the frame (slow motion), stops, and starts back down. Somewhere about this point we could use a moving-camera shot, looking down at the surface of the water and zooming toward it, then a shot taken from water level looking at the diver as he hits the water. At the editing stage, let the water come most of the way up as high as it will go, then cut to another shot, from water level, of a hugh splash in progress. You can now complete the sequence with many details of the water coming down on the dry people. This can most easily be done by having someone offscreen throw a bucket of water on each of the shots you make. They can all be cut together using match-action techniques to create a sequence that will read as a single, very large, very long splash.

The expansion of time achieved in this sequence was the result of simply stringing a lot of visual details of the action together, which added up to a total time on the screen greater than such an actual event would take. Doing this allows the audience to anticipate and participate that much more. It is like one of those situations in life in which there is so much happening in so short a time that it is difficult to see it all and feel it all, and which seems in retrospect to have extended over a fairly long time.

A variation of the technique just discussed is the overlapping of an action upon itself. In the sequence of felling a giant redwood tree, the actual fall and crash to the ground, when seen on the screen, is apt to be disappointing as it contains very little of the gigantic sense of *fall* that is felt when you are there in person. By shooting the fall from different angles, and with different lenses (using a multiple-camera setup) or by shooting various aspects of different trees falling (negating the need for more than one camera), you will have the footage to make a falling sequence of vaster power and interest. In practice, the tree might be allowed to fall a little in the first shot, and in the next to fall a little farther, and so on. Each shot could be started with the tree having fallen a little farther than it had at the *start* of the previous shot, and could be carried to where it had fallen a little farther than it had at the *end* of the previous shot. Thus, in overlapping degrees, the tree will fall, but with a sort of filmic majesty befitting the magnitude of the action. It should be realized that whenever practical examples of a filmic principal are given, by no means is the use of the principle limited to situations similar to that of the example. The principle of extending the time of an action by overlapping extra pieces of itself has almost unlimited application, from someone breaking into a smile to an airplane taking off.

The *compression* of filmic time usually requires that parts of an action be omitted, and substituted in their place a "cutaway" shot that lasts a much shorter time than the action omitted. Thus, if we have a shot of a pretty girl walking from her car to the supermarket—which might take ten seconds of screen time—we can, instead, cut out six seconds of the middle of the shot, and insert only three seconds of a man looking at her. In this manner she can be moved from her car to the market in a total time of only seven seconds. The missing three seconds of her walking will never be noticed by the audience at all. They have seen her walking toward the market, then a shot of the man looking at her, then one of her entering the market, and it all looks very normal and smooth. By this device a great deal of otherwise dead screen time can be cut out, without any sacrifice of smoothness or natural illusion. The rate of the action can be controlled with great precision and incidents made to move along either briskly or at a normal pace or at a much slower one. Cutaway shots can just as easily be used for expanding screen time, by adding more time length of cutaways than was removed from the main line of action.

Cutaways can also be used to cover a multitude of editing impasses. It frequently happens that an important part of an action is missing. Perhaps there was an oversight in the confusion of shooting, or, in documentary filming, the camera man might have been looking the wrong way or had just run out of film. Without a cutaway to cover the gap in the action, there would be a very annoying break in the flow, as though someone had snipped a couple of feet out of the film. This "jump" cut is usually found in profusion in home movies, where it is hardly less annoying than in professional films. In our example of the girl walking, we deliberately got into a jump-cut situation when we removed the middle of the shot and kept only the begining and the end. Then we solved it quite neatly by inserting the cutaway shot of the man looking at her. This time let us suppose that you feel you need the first part of her walk, and then you want to get her quickly into the market, but you don't want to use a cutaway to anything else. You could use a cutaway to her. Simply make a fairly closeup shot of her walking, either from the side or maybe head on—it could be a tracking shot of just her feet walking, her purse swinging, or her face—and insert this shot in the middle. The key requirement of a cutaway is that it be different enough in viewpoint or subject, that the time and place reference points in the scene of the main action be temporarily dropped, allowing the audience to accept the return of the main action after the cutaway at nearly any time and place you want.

Compression of time is often achieved by clever match-action cutting, dispensing entirely with the cutaway to cover the omitted time, and relying instead on such forceful and smooth matching of a strong motion at the end of one scene to the beginning action of the next scene that the audience is swept smoothly into the new time and place. For example, a conversation concludes with one man getting up and walking by just in front of the camera lens (cut); his car pulls across the screen at the same speed and same image size, so that we have saved a lot of time getting him on his way by making a formally smooth and forceful match-action cut.

Another way of manipulating apparent time is to make either an unusually large number of cuts per minute or very few. Using the example of the girl getting out of her car and walking to the market, suppose we shot so many different angles and views of her action that we could edit

By matching the screen direction and velocity of the movements of the girl and the car, as well as their light tone, a very smooth and almost magical transformation takes place.

the sequence in real time (a total of ten seconds) but cut each second to a different shot. Thus we would have ten different aspects of her action presented in rapid succession, and although time would not be compressed, it would still seem to be going very fast. Cutting the sequence this way will produce a sense of agitation and expectation in the audience. It is clear that the rapid cutting may do nothing toward revealing anything significant about her getting from the car to the market, but it does have an emotional preparatory effect, and could be a very effective technique for leading into something that requires this preconditioning for fullest impact.

The relationship between what a film-maker does when he photographs and when he edits has by now been revealed as very intimate. The separation of camera work and editing techniques is merely one of convenience, and in no way means that one can be fulfilled without the other. What shots are taken are greatly determined by what the intended editing structure of the film will be, and what editing structures you are able to use are limited to what you had the foresight to shoot. When the proposed editing structure cannot be planned in advance, which is very often the case, it is imperative to shoot enough cutaways and enough extra angles so that there will be a maximum flexibility at the editing stage to put together the footage in whatever editing structure will be most effective.

12

slow, fast, and reverse motion

Slow-motion photography is a useful and versatile technique that could be exploited far more than it is. We have all seen its use in sporting-events films, where the beautiful motion of a pole vaulter is slowed down to about half its normal speed so that we can see all the details of the muscles and limbs, the flexing of the pole, the skillful rollover at the top of the bar, and the fall into the sawdust. Slow-motion photography is often used as an engineering tool to study high speed occurrences at less than a thousandth of their normal speed. The use of slow motion in theatrical films has been very limited although the technique has great expressive power. In a Japanese film, *Seven Samurai,* two samurai are in combat with swords, and because of the slow-motion rendering, the danger in the blades is heightened as their gleaming, sharp edges slice smoothly at each other. The motions and tactics of the two highly skilled swordsmen are clearly seen, and appear as beautiful as a ballet, as their sword strokes are slowed down in keeping with the rest of the action, allowing the audience time to see a sword stroke coming and feel suspense as to whether the combatant will be able to duck or to parry it in time.

In the American film *2001,* mentioned earlier, an ape man idly hits a pile of animal bones with a large bone he is using as a club. As he discovers his club's powerful effect on the bones, he begins hitting harder and harder, causing them to fly up into the air. Instead of faster cutting to aid the sense of excited frenzy at this point, the film goes into extreme slow motion combined with very skillful match-action cutting, giving an effect of increased wonder at the discovery of the increased power the club gives the ape man as compared with his bare fist, and then, as he begins demolishing the skulls that lie on the ground around him, the camera, up very close and at ground level, sees skull after skull of mighty animals crack, split, collapse and disintegrate under the blows of early man, who, through the power of mind, has begun his pattern of domination over all the creatures of the earth. The conveyance of a complex idea and a powerful emotion in this brief sequence is due to a combination of carefully chosen factors, of which the most important is the slow motion. It has long been a tradition to use slow motion in sequences representing dreams, but it might well be pointed out that in an important sense motion pictures are all dreams.

In the silent comedies, fast motion was a universal means of making things look ludicrous and of staging very narrow escapes without undue danger of actually killing an actor. It is sometimes hard to ascertain whether the intrinsic nature of fast motion is humorous or whether it has been a matter of audience conditioning through its use in so many comedy films. It is certainly true that to intercut a fast-action piece of motion into an otherwise normal speed sequence calls attention to itself and makes the scene read as silly. The use of fast motion has become a cliché for filming something you want to make fun of, since it forces the audience into a peculiar objectivity—one of the prerequisities for humor. This objectivity seems to occur because actions such as talking, eating, laughing, walking, hitting things, falling, and so on, start, stop, and finish before we have any time to get emotionally involved with them. Fast motion has just the opposite effect of slow motion, which allows us time to see everything and to go through changes of feeling and empathy. In summary, it seems as though when film time goes slowly we become involved in myriads of visual details and feel a sense of wonder, and when filmic time goes fast we pull back and see all the outward patterns and feel a sense of humor.

Reverse motion has hardly been used creatively at all other than in comedies. Reverse motion does magic tricks very easily; it can quickly assemble a scattering of broken glass into a milk bottle, or cause a charred straw hat to spring into flame and unburn itself into brand-new condition. It has the ability to put things back as they were. It might be interesting to use this quality of reverse motion in the dramatic context of a person who was continually doing things he regretted, and who tried so hard to undo them that for just an instant or two they would indeed start to go back as they had been—then reality would pulse back into dominance, and the film would again continue in forward motion.

There are many cases in which, when an action is reversed, it is no longer the same action running backward, but is a *different kind* of action running forward. Imagine a dinner party in which food comes out of the mouths onto the forks, and is then piled up on the plates. In the proper context such a sequence would go beyond being revolting or funny. Intercut with a politician spewing forth the same old promises it would become an extensive metaphor.

It is also possible to stage an action *backward*, and then film it in reverse motion, so that it comes out forward. This produces actions which, although they are going forward, have a very strange look and feel about them. A very simple example would be to have an actor walk backward *away* from a situation he did not want to get into, but to film this in reverse. He will then be going toward the undesired situation, but his bodily movements will look unnatural, and he will seem to be trying to go the other way, thus giving visual expression to his emotional state of mind, his reluctance to go forward.

The mechanical techniques for accomplishing slow motion depend almost entirely on the built-in facilities of the camera. Assuming a normal running speed of 24 fps for 16mm and 35mm cameras, an action will be slowed down to half its speed by shooting at 48 fps. This is based on the principle that an action lasting one second will then consume 48 frames, and since the projector speed is always 24 fps, it will take two seconds for that 48 frames to be projected. The faster we run the camera, the more individual frames of a given action we will have, and the longer that action will take to unfold during projection. An exposure correction has to be made when shooting in slow motion, since each frame will be behind the lens for a shorter time due to the higher running speed, and thus will receive less exposure to light. The change in exposure is exactly proportional to the change in running speed. If you run the camera at 48 fps you will need to double the T-stop opening of the lens to compensate for each frame's being exposed only half as long. Let us take a practical situation. You are shooting at a T stop of 5.6 and want to run the camera at three times normal speed. Since this reduces exposure to one-third, you need to open the lens up three times brighter than it was. Opening up to T 4 would double the light, and opening up to T 2.8 would give four times the exposure, so the correct lens setting would be halfway between T 4 and T 2.8. On some cameras with built-in exposure systems, changing the camera running speed automatically changes the lens setting, but usually the exposure compensation would have to be made manually.

When shooting fast motion the same principles apply. Running at 12 fps will cut the screen time to half and thus double the apparent rate of speed of the action, and will also require *reducing* the lens opening to half its original opening.

The mechanics of reverse-motion filming are a bit more involved, partly because there is more than one way to do it, depending on what equipment you are using. If the camera will run backward (many fine cameras will not), then you put a cap on the lens and run the film forward for whatever length of film you think you will need for your backward shots. The lens cap prevents the film from being exposed at all. Then you simply put the camera motor in reverse and film normally, being careful not to run back onto scenes you have already taken earlier when you were running forward. It is sometimes a good idea to avoid

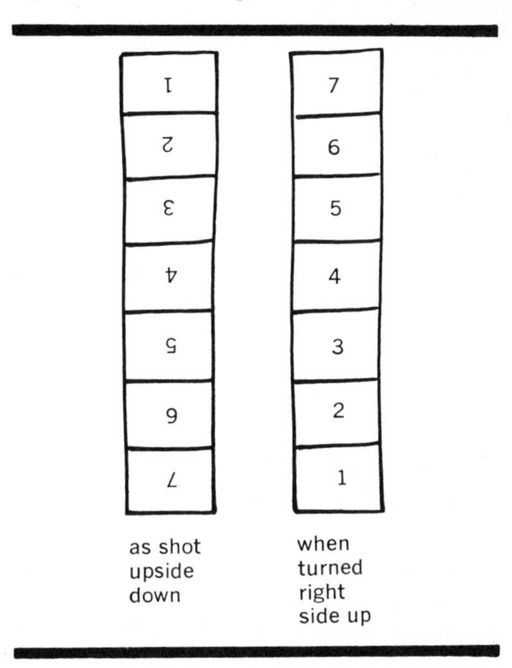

mixing forward and reverse shooting on the same roll, since it is so easy to make a mistake and ruin good footage with an unintentional overlap.

If you are using a camera that is not designed for running backward, then you will have to shoot with the camera running forward, but held upside down. This is sometimes difficult, especially if the shot requires that the camera be mounted on a tripod, but it is a problem that you can work out. When you are editing your film and come to the upside-down portion, simply turn it right side up, which, because it reverses the order of the frames, causes the scene to progress backward.

If you are using 8mm film, there is a difficulty, because of the sprocket holes along one edge of the film only; when you turn your upside-down scene to right side up, the position of the sprocket holes will have reversed, and this scene will therefore not go through the projector. (In 16mm and 35mm this is not a problem because there are sprocket holes down both sides of the film.) In order to get the sprocket holes in 8mm on the right side you can flip the strip of film over left to right, but this puts the emulsion on the opposite side of the film in comparison with the emulsion position on the forward part of the film. This means that when the reverse scene comes along it will be slightly out of focus on the screen, due to the shift in emulsion position. The only way this is avoidable is to take the extreme measure of filming your entire film with the camera upside down, thus allowing all the shots to be turned right side up in a compatible emulsion position. Those scenes in which you desired to have the motion go forward would therefore have had to be staged backward.

This is likely, however, to result in such a mind tangle that you will either go berserk or come up with a very unusual and individual film.

If you are using a projector which will run backward you can get a lot of experience in reverse motion by looking at all the footage you can lay your hands on with the projector running in reverse. You will find that most things don't look much better or worse, but that some do look interesting and will give you good filmic ideas. This way you can find out what sort of things work well in reverse without wasting a lot of film.

13

animating real objects

By means of single-frame animation, objects may be made to move about in any direction, and at any speed, entirely on their own. A sandwich can make itself out of the tidbits in the refrigerator, mechanical parts can unscrew themselves from a machine and run away, and human beings can perform strange-looking feats of locomotion.

Single-frame animation means running the camera one frame at a time, and making rearrangements of your subject matter before taking each frame. When you have taken that frame, you then make whatever change in your subject you want, and then take another frame. This process continues until you have accumulated enough frames for your purpose. Since 24 frames per second will be put through the projector, a ten-minute film by this method would require taking 14,400 frames. This is time-consuming but it is well within the realm of practicability, as witnessed by the multitude of cartoons that exist.

When single-frame filming is done with rather long intervals between frames, it is called time-lapse photography. Thus a rose can be seen blooming, unfolding its petals, and withering away. This requires the use of a mechanical device with a timer in it that will automatically trip the camera shutter at whatever time intervals it is set for, through a range of about one second to one hour. Such devices are called intervalometers, and can be rented from the same places that rent cameras. If you wanted a shot of a farmhouse and its activities for one day to be compressed into ten seconds you would need 240 frames, spaced out at even intervals of the 24 hours in a day, a time interval between frames of six minutes. This would give you ten frames per hour, or 240 frames for the 24-hour day. In the finished shot the sun would pop up, the people would rush out of the house and milk the cows, drive the pickup truck away and back, eat lunch, hang the wash out to dry, feed the chickens, eat dinner, watch the TV set, turn the lights out, go to bed and sleep till dawn, all in the same time it takes you to read this description. A very amusing film was made using this technique, of a Midwestern college football game. You saw the people pouring into the stadium, filling it up as fast as rice into a bowl, the game proceeding at furious speed, half-time bands marching around, the rest of the game, the shadows rapidly lengthening at the end of the day, and finally all the cars trying to get out of the parking lot at the same time. The entire three-hour event was compressed into a few minutes, and the effect was both funny and fascinating.

Let us suppose you want to make an animation sequence of a lawn-mower mowing the lawn by itself. The first thing to do is imagine how fast you want the mower to go. If it would normally be pushed the length of a 50-foot lawn in twenty seconds, and you would like it to go twice normal speed, then you are dealing with traversing 50 feet in ten seconds. Ten seconds of film will be 240 frames, so you divide up the 50 feet into 240 segments and arrive at the figure of about 2.4 inches of mower travel per frame. Doing the calculation in reverse, in order to check it, you figure you will move the mower 2.4 inches after taking each of the 240 frames, which would be a total distance of 48 feet—close enough to 50 feet. (It would require an error of at least 30 percent to make any noticeable difference. Smaller variations in running speed than that are not perceptible.)

Now you can set the camera up overlooking the lawn. It is necessary to use a tripod; the camera must remain steady so that the stationary background of each shot will not jump around. An assistant can take one frame, while you stand out of frame, then you go in and move the mower about 2½ inches ahead and the assistant takes another frame, and so on all over the lawn, around the bushes, in square-dance patterns, and even up a tree and back down. This last feat can be accomplished with nylon fishing line, hoisting the mower up into the tree 2.4 inches per frame as before. If you want to change camera angles during the action, there is no difference in technique from that of normal shooting. It might be a good idea to get some cutaways, perhaps of a neighbor's reactions, as they certainly have come come out to see this unusual lawnmower in action.

Perhaps one of the most interesting things to animate is human beings. There is no limit to the variations of posture and locomotion that may be imposed by animation. In a recent student film, a man drives along a grassy field in an entirely imaginary car. He sits on the ground, scooting smoothly along, steering right and left with an imaginary steering wheel, zooming a quarter of a mile away in two seconds and coming back in three to an instantaneous stop. He then attaches a tail rudder to his girl friend, who is lying face down on the grass. After spreading her arms out wide to serve as wings, he attaches a long string to her waist, and proceeds to make her taxi along the ground, and sure enough, she takes off, whirling in circles over his head on the end of the tether string he is holding. The audiences which have seen this film have screamed with delight at what can be done with imaginative use of real object animation. (The techniques involved in making her appear to fly go beyond those of animation.)

Another interesting animation to try is causing a person to walk on air. You set the camera up on a tripod, have your actor jump up about a foot off the ground, and when he is just at the peak of his jump, take a frame. Then your actor can step forward about a foot and jump again. Once more you take a frame just at the top of his jump. He can do this over all kinds of terrain, including going up and down stairs, over packing crates, even automobiles. Since all your frames were taken when your actor was a foot up in the air, he will never be seen to touch the ground.

Although animation tends to lend itself most easily to comedic situations, it can be used effectively in other contexts as well. Whenever the subjective viewpoint of a character (or of the film maker) could be represented by an unusual physical occurrence, then real object animation should be considered. Furniture might shift its position very slightly in the room, or the walls might be closing in ever so slightly, or a cigarette might be smoking with unusual vigor, or facial expressions might appear to change in a manner that at once shows both the intended façade and the hidden feeling. Real-object animation accomplishes such effects with relatively small effort and cost.

14

superimposed images

A superimposed image is one that is placed over another image, and is commonly called a double exposure. The making of composite images may involve any number of separate exposures, and may be done either in the camera while you are doing the original photography or by printing together images that were filmed separately. We will first take a look at what can be done with superimposed images, and then go into the techniques for accomplishing them.

The world of superimposed images is very different from the worlds of filmic construction we have been exploring so far. It is a world in which things do not happen one at a time, but happen simultaneously. When a complex story or theme is being unfolded, we are no longer required to switch from one scene to another, or from one subject's place in time to its next place in time. We can deal with a number of points in time all at once, or with a number of different subjects all at once, putting them on top of each other according to their thematic relationships. The analogies between filmic structure and musical structure are numerous and often illuminating. We might consider the assembling of shots together in a sequence as a musical melody in which it is the progression from note to note that is dominant. The pattern made by a long string of notes (or images) is the melody (or story). But when we play more than one note at a time, we move into the new world of harmony. When we present more than one image at a time we are making filmic chords, and it is the riches of this extra dimension that we are after now.

We presented an interesting experiment to a college class in filmmaking. We threaded up two projectors with very dissimilar film sequences and projected the images on top of each other, just to see what good things would happen. One of the most provocative results was the combination of a film of a very pregnant woman contemplatively awaiting the birth of her baby, with a sequence of a harried man in a gray flannel suit, carrying a briefcase, rushing frantically up the down escalator. Most of the shots of the woman are in fairly large closeups, while those of the man are in small-figure long shots. The contrast between the serene calmness of the woman with child and the frenzy of the man caught in a success game is a powerful one. The imagination of the audience is stimulated. How has the man gone from being born into a world of maternal care and security into a ratrace where there is no care except for oneself, and where security is forever pursued and never attained? Because his image on the screen is so small, and the woman's so large, we get the impression that he is her child already born and already propelled into a future far removed from that envisioned by a prospective mother. When the woman's body, her breast and thighs filling the screen, is superimposed upon the small figure of the man trying to run back up the escalator, there is the strong suggestion that what he is trying to reach is not the next rung on the success ladder, but to return to a state of infant bliss in the image of mother Earth, and the escalator is seen as the irreversible force of time, carrying him away from his desires.

The effect of the superimposition of the images described is totally different from that of intercutting the material of the two sequences. Intercutting them would be quite successful in making an effective contrast between the woman's and man's state of mind, but it is only through the superimposition that the strong emotional relationship between the man and the woman is expressed. The superimposition not only contrasts but at the same time synthesizes the two people into a single emotional statement.

An especially beautiful use of superimposure in a recent experimental film, *Sweet Visions*, begins with a young couple blowing soap bubbles. They become entranced with the shimmering color and airy lightness of the bubbles and imagine that it would be fun to get in one and see what they could see. At this point the realistic closeup of one of the bubbles begins to grow in size, as though the viewer were moving into it, and yet, at the same time, the bubble is seen just as it was before. We have both the real bubble, which was the basis for their fancy, and the imagined bubble, which we are entering. Then, very smoothly, multitudes of bubbles materialize in diferent glowing colors, until we are in a sea of weightless light, which then begins to fragment into varicolored points of light undulating against a jet-black background. The silhouettes of a man and woman smoothly materialize into being and sway as though under water. The two figures move freely in space and *through* each other, one of them now glowing magenta, and the other blue-green. Where their bodies overlap it is black, and the whole scene is encased in a gigantic shimmering bubble, which fades away, as does the girl, leaving the man's figure flowing in a field of twirling yellow light.

This sequence is composed of four sets of images, all exposed on the same roll of film in the camera. After the first set of images was filmed, the film was rewound back to the starting place, and the next set of exposures made on top of the first, and so on until all the elements were combined. The original bubble was photographed against a black background for the desired amount of time, then the variable shutter of the camera was gradually closed, causing the image to fade out to black. Then the film was rewound to the starting place, and while the variable shutter was being gradually opened, the bubble was slowly moved toward the camera lens. This shot was continued past the point where the first bubble faded out, and then was itself faded out. The film was then rewound several seconds in length, and then more bubbles were filmed on top of the one we appeared to move into. This last group of bubbles was then slowly faded out and the film rewound several seconds back onto itself again. Using a telephoto lens and a camera running speed of 48 fps, plus a blue filter over the lens, the reflection of the sun was filmed on the surface of undulating water, deliberately underexposed enough so that the water itself did not show, and only the brilliant colored point of light moving languorously left and right across the screen was visible.

The film was then rewound most of the way back toward the beginning of that shot, and a second exposure was made in the same manner as the first except that the camera was turned on its side, so that the motion of the light would go up and down the screen forming a cross-pattern with the first exposure; and in the second shot, a yellow filter was used to give the light a saturated color.

The roll of film in the camera was next rewound back to the beginning of the undulating lights, and a scene was filmed of the girl moving in silhouette against a white wall (the exposure techniques required for this were discussed in Chapter 6). A magenta filter was used during this shot, which turned the white wall magenta but had no effect on the girl's figure in black silhouette. The film was rewound to start of the girl's shot, and the man's moving figure was also shot in silhouette, but this time using a blue-green filter. This shot of the man was extended beyond the end of the girl shot, was then rewound several seconds in length, and a shot was faded in on top of it with a yellow light bulb with a little metal spinner going between the lamp and the camera, and a large glass multifaceted prism in front of the lens. Now, all that remained to be added was the single large bubble that the couple floated in. An ordinary soap bubble, lit from the sides and placed close enough to the lens to fill the frame, was shot against a black background and superimposed over the appropriate section. This completed the photography and editing of the entire sequence.

An interesting variation of superimposure technique is to make a visual tapestry of dissolves from one shot to the next. An event such as a

A triple exposure combining the two figures and the shimmer of a soap bubble.

large gathering of people celebrating spring with costumes and bells, guitars, picnic lunches, and frolicking serves as an example. The variable shutter on the camera is left closed; when you are framing a shot you want, start the camera running, at the same time opening up the shutter in a second or two. Within two or three more seconds you can close down the shutter and stop the camera. Gathering interesting glimpses of what is going on can be continued in this manner until you have a roll of film containing multitudes of shots that fade in for a few seconds and then fade out. These glimpses can be considered in rhythmic terms as pulses of image, with pulses of blank space between them. If you now rewind this footage and do the same thing again on top of what you have already filmed, by random chance at least half of the pulsing shots made during the *second* exposure will fall into the blank spaces left on the roll between the pulses of the first set of exposures. Wherever the fade *in* of a new scene is superimposed over the fade *out* of a previous scene, the transition will take the form of a smooth dissolve from one scene into the next. This dissolving effect itself is commonly seen in theatrical films, where it often is used to denote the passage of time. There may be a passage in which the pioneers are planting corn, and as the camera lingers on a shot of the planted field, the shot dissolves into a shot of the same field several weeks later when all the corn shoots are up and growing. Although this kind of dissolve and the dissolves we made in the image-pulsing sequence above are mechanically the same (superimposure of a fade-in over a fade-out), the effect is vastly different. In the pulsing sequence what happens *during* the dissolve is as important as what precedes and follows it. The rhythmic interplay of all the various shots is experienced as beautiful variations of the same spirit, continually taking on new forms in smooth and rapid succession.

From these examples it can be seen that superimposure can be used to combine pictorial and subject elements into whatever visual relationships the film-maker can imagine. If he wants his sky to have billowy white clouds in it he can superimpose them in. A person in a story can be behaving outwardly in one manner while a superimposure shows him as he really feels. For example, suppose we have a closeup of a woman being told something she wants very much to hear, but she has to pretend it is bad news. A very faint shot of her face breaking into a smile can be superimposed over her outward face, in exact register, and then faded away. Our impression will be one of having momentarily able to see into her true state of mind. Visual metaphors can be superimposed on the realistic subjects they refer to. A shot of a man who feels that the bottom has just dropped out of his world can be superimposed onto a shot made with the camera falling down a well. A person who feels claustrophobic about the city could be shown being forced into a smaller and smaller space (perhaps a corner of the screen?) by superimposed skylines of the bulk of the city moving in on him. A person feeling expansive out of some great joy can be shown as several images of himself all starting from a central position and expanding out to all corners of the screen. Fireworks, waterfalls, birds in flight, masses of people, flames, demolition, parachutes and so on are samples of the kind of pictorial material especially effective in superimposures, because it expresses feeling as strongly as it expresses its own physical nature. Such a thing as a train may seem like a good visual metaphor for a situation which cannot be steered in any other direction (railroaded), but somehow it will not read that way in a film; it will most often stubbornly insist on being a train regardless of what the film-maker wants us to make of it. Finding images that will work as metaphors is not difficult but it does take care. Simply because you, the film-maker, know what some image means to you, is no guarantee that it will have the same meaning for an audience. One of the most important abilities a film-maker must develop is being able to put himself in the audience's place and see his meanings as they will see them presented on the screen. The film-maker must find pictures that express feelings and meanings, rather than merely imitating the playwright and having pictures of actors *saying* what the feelings and meanings are. The film-maker can make great use of the crafts of writing and acting, but these are only part of film's great potentiality for expression.

We must also understand the basic technical principles of making usable superimposed images. The physical nature of the photographic emulsion is such that light exposed to it in subsequent exposures may have additive effect, but it does not subtract from the previous exposure level. This means that after having photographed a desert sand dune as the background for a superimposed title, you could not make a second exposure of black title letters on top of this. The actual black letters that you are trying to photograph are black because they reflect no light. Therefore the image of the letters formed by the camera lens on top of the previous exposure of the sand dune will not further effect the film emulsion. All that may happen is that the negative space around the black letters, which would be a lighter tone, would add a little further exposure to the sand dune background in the area *around* the letters, thus washing out the detail of the sand and making it appear overexposed. We can very easily superimpose title letters over the sand-dune shot if the letters are lighter than the dunes. In other words, we can add the letters to the dunes because we can *add* light to the exposure in the shape of the letters. We cannot make any area of the frame darker by superimposures, only lighter.

In making multiple exposures in the camera it makes virtually no difference whether the film being used is negative or reversal. But when the multiple exposure will be made by combining separate shots in a laboratory printing process the principles are different. For example, if you shoot a white title on a black background, using negative film in the camera, the processed negative will contain opaque letters on a clear field. The light beam used in the printing machine will expose the print stock all around the shape of the opaque letters, thus obliterating whatever other picture material you are trying to multiple print with it. However, since the title letters on the negative you are printing from are opaque, whatever picture material you multiple print will show up in the print contained in the shape of the title letters. This can be a very exciting visual effect. You could even shoot a roll of single-frame animated white shapes on a black background (using negative stock in the camera) and then multiple print this with some live action footage (also shot on negative stock). This would result in the live action footage appearing only in the shapes of the animated (originally white) material, and this would appear on a black background.

Since the making of two exposures on one piece of film would seem to double the amount of exposure on that film, it might be thought that giving each of the two exposures one-half its normal value would then yield a total exposure of the correct value. This is true only under certain conditions. It must be remembered that a correct exposure is one that looks good to you. Superimposing one image over another usually looks best if both are given an exposure appropriate to your intent, rather than an exposure one-half of "normal." If every part of the frame area of the second exposure were the same brightness as the corresponding spot in the first exposure, then the two exposures would double. But this very rarely happens. What we are more likely to have is a complicated pattern of many shades of light and dark (a picture, in other words) superimposed upon a different pattern of light and dark, and for most of the picture area there will be no doubling of exposure.

We can make great use of the fact that dark areas of an exposure have no effect (do not show) on subsequent exposures. In the example given of a man falling down an endless well we are interested only in the body of the man in the exposure concerning him, and we want to eliminate his environment entirely so that

A double exposure made by sandwiching two strips of film together and printing through them. Unlike double exposures made in the camera, this results in the dark areas remaining opaque.

it will not conflict with the environment of the well shaft onto which we intend to superimpose him. This can most easily be done by filming the man against a black background, either in a dark studio with selective lighting on him alone, or outdoors at night, if no studio is available. In preparing the shot of the well, it would be helpful to set it up so that the center area of the frame is fairly dark; the man will then superimpose quite nicely on it. By controlling your light and dark areas in each of the superimposed shots, you can heighten the effect you want, concentrating on only those elements important to your theme. It should be noted that when you make two or more exposures on a single piece of film the amount of picture information piled up together is apt to be quite confusing. It is usually best to combine single key elements, one in each of the exposures, with a photographic simplicity allowing as little *extraneous* picture material in each shot as possible.

The synchronization of any given frame in one exposure with a given frame of another exposure is not often necessary. None of the examples of this chapter required it. But suppose something should happen in one of the exposures just at the exact frame in a previous exposure where somebody sneezes. This can best be accomplished by photographing the two events on separate strips and combining them in the editing assembly (see Chapter 20). At this stage the two strips of film may be lined up side by side with exact relation between frames as desired; then the two can be printed together onto one strip in the laboratory.

Using a zoom lens to make multiple exposure shots can produce some very interesting results. Suppose you make a shot of a person, and during the shot you change the zoom lens slowly from a wide-angle position into a telephoto position. Then after winding the film back, you make a second shot of the same person, but this time you slowly change the zoom lens from telephoto position to wide-angle position. The resulting shot will show a large image of the person superimposed over a small image of him, and as the superimposed zooms progress the large image will shrink as the small image grows. Spatially they will seem to pass through each other. The apparent motions and changes of image size which can be obtained with a zoom lens render it an especially versatile tool in combination with multiple images.

15

special visual effects

It is often important to make closeup shots of very small objects such as wristwatches, eyes, a needle being threaded, fingerprints, granulated sugar, the end of a cigarette, the face of a bee—and since the closest distance to which a normal lens will focus is only about a foot or two, we have a problem getting close enough for the subject to fill the entire screen. A supplementary closeup lens may be attached to the front of the camera lens, and with this, distances of down to about six or eight inches may be focused upon. Such closeup lenses come in different optical strengths, which are indicated by their diopter number—the larger the number, the closer the lens may be focused. These lenses are relatively inexpensive and come with instruction sheets giving the details of their use. For closeups in the distance mentioned above, such a closeup lens is the easiest solution. It may be attached and detached very quickly, and requires no compensation for exposure in its use. For closer closeups you will need a device called an extension tube. This is merely a piece of tubing, threaded on both ends, which is screwed into the camera body, upon which the lens is then mounted. This makes the effective distance between the lens and the film plane greater, bringing objects only a tiny distance in front of the lens into sharp focus. Extension tubes come in sets so that you have a choice of magnification powers. A typical set for a 16mm camera would have a 5mm, 10mm, 20mm and 40mm tube. By using these in different combinations you have increments of 5mm available from 5mm through 75mm. With the whole set being used at once on a 25mm lens, you can fill the screen with one letter of type from this page. Sometimes it is difficult to get the camera right up close to your subject. In this case you can use the extention tubes with a telephoto lens, enabling you to put the camera several inches farther away from the subject and still maintain the very close view. Since the use of extension tubes changes the effective focal length of the lens used, the effective T stop is also altered, and for this reason the lens must be opened wider to make up for the loss of efficiency. The corrected T stop setting may be calculated by the formula

$$\left(\frac{\text{length of extension tube (in mm)}}{\text{focal length of lens used (in mm)}} + 1\right)^2 = \begin{matrix}\text{numerical} \\ \text{increase in} \\ \text{exposure}\end{matrix}$$

For example, suppose the use of a length of extension tube 25mm long, on a lens 25mm in focal length. Applying the formula to this information gives 25 divided by 25, yielding 1, and to this is added 1, yielding 2; this quantity is squared, yielding a numerical increase of 4 required for proper exposure. To increase the exposure four times would require opening the lens two more T stops, since opening it one stop would double the light passed, and opening it another stop would double that again, giving an increase of four. At extremely close distances camera jiggle becomes intolerable, and so a steady tripod must be used. The depth of field focus becomes extremely shallow, making use of a reflex-type camera mandatory. The depth of field may be made deeper by using the smallest T stop opening you can manage and compensating for this by putting very bright light right up close to your subject. It takes care to handle all of these technical matters in making extreme closeups, but it is worth the often astounding results.

When a shot of something going on suddenly stops and becomes motionless, then later springs back into motion, the effect is called a freeze frame. This is done by selecting the desired frame out of the strip of film of the action and making a copy of it on another strip of film that extends for any number of frames desired. If you want to stop a diver in mid-air for three seconds, you film the shot normally and have it processed. Then you look at the shot and select the frame you want to freeze. An optical laboratory can then reprint that one frame 72 times down a strip of film; when you splice that piece into the middle of your diving shot, the frame you select will be repeated 72 times (three seconds), and then the action will continue. In order to save the rather high cost of having this done by a laboratory, you can make a freeze-frame sequence by mounting the selected frame solidly in front of a bright, diffused light source and rephotographing it with a motion-picture camera. Since photographing a single frame of motion-picture film amounts to an extreme closeup, even in 35mm, you will need to use the closeup techniques just described. It is very difficult to determine the exact exposure required, since the single frame is too small to take a reliable reading on. Since a freeze frame involves using such a small length of film, it would be best to make several runs, each at a different exposure setting.

It is quite simple to make a subject appear instantly in the middle of a scene and then instantly disappear. The camera must be set up on a tripod and the shot of the environment made. The camera is then stopped, and whatever is to appear is placed in view. The camera is then run again until you want the subject to disappear. The subject is then removed and the shot finished with only the environment. If you are using a camera that will stop quickly with the shutter closed you will probably not even need to do any cutting of the sequence later. With cameras that stop gradually or have shutters that do not always stop in the closed position, you need only assemble the usable portions of the three sections when you are editing. You might have a shot in which a person is running along, instantly vanishes for a while, and then instantly reappears, still running, right where he had vanished.

Making subjects appear and disappear gradually is somewhat more involved. This involves shooting the environment and the subject separately in a superimposition. Let us suppose you want a girl to walk along in a white robe, dematerialize as she goes through a solid wall, and then rematerialize on the other side. The shot of the wall can be made first, with an effort at keeping the area in which the girl is to superimpose fairly dark. Then the girl must be shot against a black background. The choice of white robe was largely to make the double exposure work better, for reasons discussed in Chapter 14. As she approaches the area of the frame where the wall was in the first exposure, the variable shutter can be smoothly closed, causing her image to disappear just as she hits the wall. She can reappear on the other side by the reverse of the same process. The limitation of this technique is that anything of a very light tone in the environment will show right through the girl's body.

A useful variation of this technique produces appearances and disappearances of people without their being semitransparent during the shot. We will suppose a witch is to materialize in the middle of the room in a matter of three seconds. We put the camera on a tripod so that it will not move, and we make a shot of the room, at the end of which we gradually close the variable shutter, causing the scene to fade out to black in three seconds. Leaving the shutter closed, the film is then wound back three seconds' worth (72 frames), the witch assumes her place in the room, and a three-second fade-in is made, causing the witch to appear at first as a dim ghost and finally to become quite solid. Although mechanically this camera technique is basically a dissolve, it requires an extra consideration if it is to work well. The camera cannot be allowed to move even the slightest between the two exposures, or you will get an out register double image of the room.

There are methods of combining separate exposures in such a way that backgrounds do not show through the foreground subjects. These are very complicated and very expensive, but an outline of the general technique may be of interest. We will set the problem of having some men discover an island on which prehistoric monsters are still living. The monsters are usually played by large tropical lizards, who have had extra fins and horns glued onto their bodies to make them look more bizarre. They are set into an environment of miniature trees and rocks and photographed from fairly close up, so that they appear to be 40 or 50 feet tall. Since the lizards' movements are too quick for such a large scale, they are filmed in some degree of slow motion. The whole effect can be quite real-looking. The problem for the film-maker comes at the point where the men and the monsters must both appear in the shots at the same time. In reality it is the men who are huge and the monsters who are small. The men can be made small by filming them from an appropriately great distance, with a background illuminated only by light of an especially narrow wavelength. In a special camera is mounted a glass prism that allows the image of the men to be photographed in the normal manner. The background is not photographed along with them, however, because the prism reflects the special light from the background off to another strip of film running in another part of the camera. This film receives light from the background only, and it yields an image which is a high-contrast negative silhouette of the moving figures of the men. If this strip of film were to be projected it would show a jet-black background with the moving *shapes* of the men clear (white on the screen). From this strip of film a duplicate is made with the tone polarities reversed, so that the images of the men appear in opaque (black) silhouette against a clear background. This "matte," as it is called, is sandwiched together with the shot of the monsters and printed onto a roll of film. If this were projected it would show the monsters in their environment, with the silhouette shapes of the men superimposed on the scene. Since this area of the frame has not been yet exposed, due to the masking effect of the matte, it will now accept an additional exposure. This exposure is made by sandwiching the shot of the men together with the other matte, which contains clear area in the shape of the men but is opaque all around them. Thus the figures of the men are printed into the blank unexposed places left for them in the print of the monsters. There are some simpler ways of achieving matte effects at little or no cost. They do not give the precise control of the method just described, but they are capable of creating unusual appearances. If you photograph anything in high-contrast silhouette, for instance a go-go girl dancing, the condition of the film emulsion before processing is such that the area of the frame consisting of the girl has not yet been exposed to light and is therefore virgin film, ready for an image. The area of the frame around the shape of the girl is fully exposed to light, and further exposure will have almost no effect on it. This means that in a subsequent re-exposure of this unprocessed film, the new image will register only on the unexposed shape of the girl and will not register on the background around her. If your second exposure had been of a crowd dancing, the final result on the screen would be a crowd of people dancing in the shape of a girl dancing, and all on a white background.

Having this effect appear on a black background instead of white is possible, but much more complicated. The girl is first filmed in silhouette on black-and-white reversal film, which when processed will yield a black figure on a white background. Then the dancing crowd is filmed on another piece of film of the *negative type.* When the lab double-prints these two images onto a single strip of *print* film (which *reverses* tones), this is what happens: The opaque shape of the girl blocks the light from the printing machine, yielding unexposed area on the print stock, in her shape, but fully exposing the area around her (causing it to come out black). Then the crowd shot is exposed on top of this. The formerly unexposed area of the print stock (in the shape of the girl) will accept the crowd shot normally. The fully exposed area around her will not accept much further exposure from the crowd shot, and thus the crowd shot will appear only in her shape. The crowd shot will print in the normal tone polarity because we shot it on negative film.

The beauty of the matte technique described above is that any subject can be made to appear in the outline shape of any other subject. Title letters, palm fronds, race cars, horses, mandalas, crosses, bridges, trees, cats, even explosions, can all be shot in either negative or positive silhouette and used as control mattes to shape the content of other shots into their own form.

There is a device called a matte box which can be mounted onto the front of a camera. It is simply a light-tight bellows with a rectangular opening at the front upon which various control elements may be mounted. A piece of black cardboard with a hole cut in it could be slipped into position on the front of the matte box so that shots taken would appear to be seen through a telescope. Mattes can be made of whatever shape is desired and an exposure made through them, yielding a shaped image on an unexposed field. Making multiple exposures with a variety of mattes, or even with the same matte shifted into different positions, can accomplish a wide variety of interesting effects. An actor can be made to appear in two places at once by matting out the left half of the frame while he is appearing in a shot at the right, and then rewinding and matting out the right side while he appears in the shot at the left. There is apt to be a very slight telltale vertical line where the two halves join, but this is often obscured by having vertical edges in the scene itself. Another procedure is to mask off the top of the frame right at an actor's neckline. The film is rewound and the bottom part of the frame, which contained the actor's body, is masked off. Now his head can be filmed in the top half, and of course it can be made to have a rather loose connection with the body.

The matte box is very convenient in situations where precise alignment of the edges of the matte and the subject matter is critical. Its main limitation is that its matting effect is stationary and has none of the tremendous flexibility of shape and motion of the photographic mattes we have been discussing.

Special color effects can be made most easily with colored gelatin filters. The range of colors available in photographic filters is quite limited, but the colors available in gelatin filters made for theatrical lighting are gorgeous and come in huge variety. If you are using a camera equipped with a behind-the-lens filter slot, very small pieces of filter material will suffice, and since it is often possible to obtain small sample books of an entire set of twenty or thirty colors, this is an inexpensive way to acquire a good set of colors without having to buy the large sheets of gelatin.

Here are some specific examples of the use of color filters along with technical considerations in their use. In the sequence described in Chapter 14 a man and woman were seen in silhouette, seemingly underwater in various colored reflections, and floating along inside a huge bubble, the effect was achieved with a superimposure of four different elements. Three of these had their color modified or supplied by color filters. The woman was photographed against a brightly lit white wall. There was no light on her body at all, so that her image is entirely black. A magenta filter was used in her shot, rendering the wall magenta, but having no effect on her figure since it reflected no light. Then the man was filmed as a superimposure on top of this shot, but in his case a blue-green filter was used. The wall has now been filmed twice, through both a magenta and and a blue-green filter, and is rendered in the final print as a pale, cool magenta. The area comprising the woman's figure is blue-green in the final print, since the blue-green wall was superimposed over it during the man's exposure. His figure is rendered as magenta, since the magenta of the wall during the woman's exposure will show on his silhouette. But where the two figures overlap, it is entirely black, since this area was never exposed to the wall light in either of the two filtered shots. The third pictorial element added was a slow-motion telephoto shot of the sun's reflection playing languorously on the surface of undulating water. These reflections were desired to appear in yellow and blue in order to match the color scheme of the soap bubbles from which the sequence evolved. The use of gelatin filters of these two colors further abstracted the appearance of the sun from its ordinary state, and contributed to the scheme of color continuity in the sequence.

In a sequence involving the temporary transformation of a girl lounging on a couch into a tempting sex queen in a very scanty costume, a color shift was called for that would make the transformation a little more colorful than real. The first part of the shot was made through a Wratten 85 daylight conversion filter, even though a color stock balanced for tungsten was already being used. This filter rendered the scene in pale salmon-orange tones, generally subduing the colors in her dress and the couch pillows. The sex queen was photographed through an intense rose-pink filter which did not inhibit the colors of her costume or the pillows, and gave a very flattering rendition of her bare skin tone.

In a sequence where a man's face slowly begins looking haggard and gaunt, then returns to normal, the first exposure of his face was made in a normal manner. The film was rewound and a deep-blue filter placed behind the lens in the camera-filter slot. The camera and the man's head had carefully maintained their exact position so that the second exposure would register exactly on top of the first. The camera was started, but with the variable shutter closed. At the right point, the shutter was slowly opened, exposing the blue face (which also had been lit very harshly for this exposure) onto the previous shot of the normal face, and then the shutter was faded out, which caused the blue effect to fade out and the face to return to normal. This resulted in a sequence with exactly the eerie transformation into a death face called for in the story.

A sequence of an Easter Be-In includes a section where a girl with bare feet, wearing an ankle-length robe, is swaying from side to side with her arms toward the sky in a sort of supplicational dance. This shot was rhythmically faded in and out in time with her dancing (by use of a variable shutter), and the film was then rewound and rhythmically faded in and out on a large fountain of water leaping into the air. This shot was done through several different color filters so that the fountains would appear in different colors, and in order to enhance the uplift effect of the water, and to have a multiplicity of waters, double exposures of the water were made in which water of one color appears to rise out of water of another color. The camera position was chosen so that a great deal of sunlight was not only shining on the water, but shining through it as well, giving a translucent glow to the colors. The camera position was also chosen to use a large dark building as a background to the shot, so that the water would by far the brightest object in the frame and thus the only element to show up in the multiple exposure with the girl. The final appearance of the sequence is very beautiful, with the girl and the jets of colored water cross-fading through each other in a sort of dance between them. The sequence ends with the gradual appearance of a large golden sun in the middle of the frame, which gets progressively brighter until it takes over the whole scene.

Color filters work by freely passing color of their own hue and rejecting, to various degrees, the passage of other colors. A piece of red gelatin looks red because it freely passes red light but tends to restrict the passage of other colors, especially those

A double exposure of the girl and a fountain.

which are complimentary to it, such as blue and green. With knowledge of this principle, a great deal can be predicted as to what effect a color filter will have on a scene. The best method for making such estimations is direct observation, as the effect of looking through the filter at the scene to be photographed will be similar to the way it will be rendered in color photography. If you want a color in a scene to be suppressed, you can use a filter which is complimentary to it. A blue shirt will be rendered almost black if you shoot it through a red filter. A blue shirt will be rendered no bluer than it appears normally if you shoot it through a blue filter. If a sequence is continued for a long while through a color filter, the mind begins to adapt to that color as being normal. If you want to maintain the sense of saturated color in a sequence, you have to provide reference points of other colors from time to time. It is when color is *compared* by the mind that it seems colorful. A color all by itself soon loses its color.

Color filters have use in black-and-white photography also. The most common use is for improving the rendition of sky, particularly where white clouds are to be emphasized. For this purpose a yellow filter can be used; this holds back some of the blue light from the sky, causing it to register darker on the film. The filter does not much affect the clouds, since they are white, and thus the relative contrast of the sky and its clouds is increased in a pictorially pleasing way. Using an orange filter increases the effect described, and a red filter produces a very stark and highly dramatic darkening of the sky. To compensate for the loss of light through the filter, the lens must be opened up one T stop for a standard yellow filter, one and a half for an orange filter, and three for a red filter.

Glass prisms which fragment the images photographed through them can be used for a wide variety of shape distortions and for multiplying a single element into many. In a sequence where a Persian brass lamp with little windows of colored glass is to be seen with heightened perception by the characters in the story, the original small points of colored light coming from the lamp begin to proliferate out into the space around the lamp, eventually filling the entire frame with shimmering jewels of light. The pattern then begins to contract back into the lamp, and it returns to normal. The lamp itself was first filmed against the black ceiling from which it hung. A second exposure was superimposed on top of this, in which a closeup shot of the lamp was fractured by filming through a multifaceted glass prism. The prism could be rotated to produce a circular pattern, but, even better, could be rolled over on its own axis so that images coming through it were alternately squeezed into a small space and then expanded out over the whole frame area. The appearance of the fracturing of an image by a prism is apt to be fairly interesting, but what is far better are the kinds of motion of the fractured pieces of the image that can be induced by appropriate motion of the prism. In selecting prisms, your eye is the best instrument, although the optical combination of the prism and the camera lens produces strong effects not visible to the eye. A reflex camera is once again your best friend.

When it is desired to soften an image into a dreamlike or romantic pictorial impression, there are readily available methods of diffusing the image. One of the most common methods used by still photographers is smearing a very light coat of petroleum jelly in circular patterns on a piece of clear glass. A small uncoated area is usually left in the very center. Shooting through this produces a sharp image in the center of the frame, and a gradually more diffuse image out toward the edges. However, this method does not work well in shots where there is much motion in the scene, or of the camera, because the smear pattern and clear spot are then objectionably evident. Another technique is to use a standard diffusion lens made by a filter company. These come in graduated strengths and produce the kind of soft-skin texture and glowing highlights seen often in romantic films of the 1930s. Another interesting diffusion device is the crosstar filter, which is available for only a few dollars. It has a cross-hatch pattern etched into it which renders light sources and specular reflections as tiny stars. This can be quite nice-looking with such subjects as candles, glassware, jewelry, sunsets, water scenes, and so on.

We have so far dwelt only on special visual effects made in the photography or printing of the image. We will now explore ultra-short cuts. If a shot were only 24 frames long, it would last one second. We could keep trimming this shorter, one frame at a time, until we ended up with the minimum length of one frame. The degree to which a scene of only one frame can be seen depends on several variables. The one frame is far more apparent if it is cut into an otherwise continuous and fairly lengthy shot. If the one frame is placed between two "normal"-length shots, it will not be seen by most of the audience, because the distraction of the long scene changing to the next long scene masks out the fact that there was one frame of something else between them. If it were desired to introduce the content of the single-frame shot below the perception threshold of most of the audience, and to then gradually increase audience awareness of this new element, the new element could be hidden between the lengthier shots, but each time it appeared it could be made one frame longer, until it demanded attention.

A further variable in the perceptibility of a single frame is the frequency of such frames in a context of a longer shot. The single frame is most perceptable when it occurs at regular intervals or in a predictable time pattern. Once the viewer catches on to the pattern, he anticipates the single-frame cut and is mentally ready for it, and thus much more able to see what it is. Even when there is merely a random scattering of single frames in a section, as long as they are occuring at intervals of not more than about five seconds they are far more noticeable than when they occur only once, all by themselves, in a context of normal-length shots. When an ultra-short cut occurs for the first time, a viewer is apt to wonder if he saw what he thinks he saw, or if there was perhaps some mistake in the mechanics. Leaving him in this state distracts him from what is being presented. When short cuts occur in groups, it is very plain that the effect is intentional and that there is a communicative reason for them.

The amount of detail that can be seen *in* a single frame shot is very little. Its color can be easily identified. If it is a familiar object, such as a tree, filmed against a plain background, it can be recognized. More complex pictorial arrangements cannot be recognized by most people. In a single frame there can be no motion to see, since it would require at least two frames for there to be any change in position of anything in the frames. When the number of frames is increased to four, such subjects as faces, animals, cars, printed words and numbers, guns, roads and large motions can clearly be seen. Rapid-fire cutting of four-frame scenes occurs at about the rate a Swiss wristwatch ticks, and while exciting for a short while, quickly becomes exhausting and causes the viewer to go numb in self-defense. Use of a section of continuous ultra-fast cutting is appropriate to such things as television commercials, which are strong attention-getters and do not last very long, but for dramatic purposes ultra-short cutting is much more effective when it is peppered into a slower context and arranged in a pattern corresponding to the intent of the dramatic context. For example, in the story of a girl haunted by the fear that negligence on her part had caused the death of her lover, the key pictorial points leading up to the death of her lover could be introduced as ultra-quick interjections into her present life. Little actions or objects might remind her of similar elements in the past that were part of the story of her lover's death, and as quickly as she would be reminded of these things, her will would force them out of her mind. This mental process could be dramatically expressed by an ever-increasing flood of ultra-quick cuts, gathering strength against her will, and threatening to destroy her shaky balance of mind.

It has been pointed out that ultra-quick cuts have little value in themselves, and that what makes them important is the *patterns* in which they are used. The major variables in the pattern are how often do they occur, in what manner do their own lengths vary, and in what way do their contents relate to the dramatic context into which they are embedded. The conclusions just presented are the result of experimental presentations in which ultra-quick cutting was presented in various patterns to an audience whose members were then queried as to what they had experienced.

16

directing non-actors

The people who appear in most films other than those made by the theatrical film industry are not professional film actors. The ways of working with people who do not have much acting experience are quite different from those used with accomplished professionals. For one thing, non-actors have not worked out ways of representing various emotional states. If asked to look surprised, they are apt to merely make a funny face, try as they may to give you what you want. Non-actors also find it very difficult to maintain an intense mood or characterization for more than a fraction of a minute. They tend to slip in and out of character, completely out of control. They also tend to get tired very quickly, because of the strain of trying to do something that is beyond their range.

All these traits, which would be a disaster for a person acting on stage, can be largely overcome in many kinds of film acting, because of the fragmentary nature of a film's shooting and editing, and because the filmmaker is right there during the performance, to help and guide.

Careful casting of the parts will solve half of the acting all by itself. In most underground, independent, avant-garde, and university films, the actors are chosen from friends and acquaintances who are interested in the film project and curious enough to try acting a part. If you need a very urbane, cool and poised young woman, it will not work at all to cast someone in the part who is not that way at all. A really good actress could play the part, regardless of what her own personality was like, but a non-actress will appear only to be hamming, no matter how hard she tries not to. If you do not know a girl who fits the part, do not try to make do with one who doesn't. Ask your friends if they know anybody who fits the description. Perhaps somebody's secretary, or sister, or a girl in a friend's dancing class will turn out to be just who you are looking for.

The next thing to do is interest the persons you'll want as actors in the film project. Tell them very briefly what your film-making credentials are, where the money is coming from to finance the film, what style of film it is, and what the part is that you think they might be very good for. If they do not respond with interest to this proposal, ask them if they would be willing to tell you why not. If they do not want to tell you, thank them for listening to your story and start looking elsewhere. If they do tell you, and you can't do anything about it (for instance, if they work in the daytime, go to school at night, and go out of town on weekends), you'll still have to look elsewhere. If you sense that they would like to do it, but are hesitant about the time and effort they would have to give, explain the shooting plan and schedule so that they'll know what's involved, and therefore be better able to make a go-ahead decision.

It is frequently helpful to arrange a screening of a sample of your previous work, so that prospective actors can be assured as to your competence. Always remember that you are asking people to do something that is probably difficult and strange to them; some of them may not even know you.

Now that the parts are all typecast, the next step is going over the plan of the film together with your actors. At present the film exists only in your head, and your actors have only a vague idea of what it is all about. After you have familiarized them with the story line, tell them all that you can about each of the personalities in your proposed film. The woman who simply cannot cope with the technologies of a very modern kitchen might be one character. Much more will have to be understood about her. Is she *afraid* of the mechanisms or is she simply bewildered by their seeming complexity? If there is a mutual hostility between her and the machines in the kitchen, then she will have to act her part differently than if she is a passive victim and very naïve. The time for your actors to understand the part they are to play is during the preshooting discussion, not during shooting.

The people who have consented to act in your film are doing so largely because they are interested in films and would enjoy being in one. Therefore they will be interested to know about the techniques you will be using during the shooting and the editing. If you plan slow motion, animation, stop action, multiple exposures, matching-action cutting or whatever, tell your new actors about it so they can participate as fully as possible in making the film. At best, it is a project-adventure which you are all embarking on together, and everything you can do to make it a mutually satisfying trip will be reflected in the quality of the finished film.

Now that the actors know your film fairly intimately, you are ready to begin shooting.

With non-actors, the film-maker's major tool of influence is the elicitation of response. This means that rather than merely telling the "actor" to smile, you must find a way to *elicit* a smile, as a natural response to something that you do. This sometimes involves a bit of trickery, so it is usually best to let your actors know why you did something, after it has already produced the response you wanted. For example, you may need a closeup of a girl breaking into a very spontaneous and pleased smile in the midst of a conversation with her lover. You might go about getting the smile by asking her to sit where she should be sitting for that shot, *before* she checks her makeup or brushes her hair. In this way the shot can be lit, and the camera prefocused and framed. Then ask her to go and give the final touches to her grooming, and when she comes back, have her sit again in the same place. You might then look at her very carefully, break into a smile and tell her that not only is what she has done what you wanted, but that she looks *very* pretty. (The camera has been running all this time.) When she breaks into a pleased smile (very likely), it will have a quality of spontaneity and warmth that she could probably never give if asked directly. Immediately after this shot is finished, you could tell her that you filmed that smile, and that it will be perfect to use in that place in the conversation where, etc., etc. Whatever slight resentment she might have at such tactics will almost certainly be swept away by your having let her in on why you tricked her, and, even more importantly, by her feeling of satisfaction and confidence in herself after having "acted" so very well.

In the chapter on editing sound, we discussed a sequence in which, during a couple's conversation, the picture cut away from the girl to the man's reaction at something she said. The shot of that reaction could probably best be gotten by some sort of elicitation of response. The camera shot could be set up on him and that section of dialogue begun. By previous arrangement between you and the girl, a line she was to say in the middle of the conversation could be dropped, and instead she could begin to say something entirely unexpected —perhaps a line from *Macbeth* or a string of profanities, or whatever might produce just the sort of look desired. This example brings up the matter of personalities, which is at the heart of the relationship between the film-maker and the people appearing in his film. To gauge just what unexpected statement by the girl will produce just what reaction by the man is an extremely intuitive matter, depending entirely on the specific personalities of the people involved. The man's reaction could be shock, confusion, laughter, anger, quizzicality, bewilderment or embarrassment. Therefore, all of these reactions (and more) could be gotten by various combinations of personalities and unexpected statements or actions. It becomes apparent at this point that the meetings of actors and film-maker that took place before shooting have a very important function beyond making plans and preparations. It is vital that the film-maker get to know the personalities of the people who will be in his film, so that he can know how and to what they will respond during shooting. In many cases the plan of the film may be changed somewhat to accommodate the personalities who will be enacting it.

There are often good reasons for changing the details of what is to be shot from what had originally been planned. One of the most important reasons is to give a sense of the action happening for the first time. Suppose you have a sequence in which the girl comes into a large room and discovers the man's body lying on the floor. Next to him is a very unfamiliar-looking metallic object. She rushes over to him and gets down to see what has happened to him, shakes him a bit, then puts her head to his chest and listens for a heartbeat. He is alive! But he will not wake up from his trance. She picks up the strange object, turns it over, starts to turn a switch on the device but very abruptly stops herself, puts it down and rushes from the room.

Now the contradiction is this: In the film she is to appear to do all this for the first time, in great distress and wonderment. But in order for you to shoot the scene, she must know all along exactly what she is to see next and do next. When she comes into the room she will, in reality, know just where he is lying, that there is an object beside him, etc. It will be very difficult for her to act as if she doesn't already know these things. It is important that she be somewhat confused, not knowing what to do next, or what the details of the strange object are. Yet the amount of planning and rehearsal necessary to shoot this scene will preclude that any of these things will provide her with an elicited response. This problem is so difficult that even experienced actors stumble over it, as you have probably seen. One of the ways of solving it, in this case, is to set up the scene with a few carefully chosen deviations from the original plan, without the girl's knowing what these are. Depending on her personality, you could tell her that when she comes into the scene things will be a little different and that she will have to find things out for herself at that point, or you might prefer to let the changes be a complete surprise to her. His body might be put on the other side of the room, so that she *will* be seeing him there for the first time. She might have been told nothing about the strange object. The original plan might have been for her to feel for a pulse at his wrist, but during the shooting the film-maker could switch and tell her out loud to put her ear to his chest for a heartbeat. She will be doing this for the first time also and will appear to have just thought of it. When she picks up the metallic object, it will be quite unfamiliar to her, and just as she is about to turn the switch on (as was planned), the film-maker yells at her not to touch that switch.

A much less complicated alternative to the above method might be to coach her by voice during the camera take, just as was done in feature films prior to sound. You could play eerie music on the phonograph if you felt is was worthwhile to carry things that far. But by the film-maker's acting out the sequence *verbally*, while she is acting it out physically, he sets up a situation of response for her rather than leave her to carry the whole thing off by herself. The film-maker's dialogue might go something like this: (Just as she glances toward the body) *Screeeeeeeeaaaam!* (She is startled and doubly alarmed) What has *happened* to him? (She rushes over) Oh, my God, he might be dead! (She wonders how to find out if he is alive and starts to pick up his wrist) No! Put your ear to his chest and listen for a heartbeat. (She suddenly thinks of how to find out) Can you hear his heart beating? (Strained attention on her face) Yes! you can! he's *alive.* (She is very glad and relieved) Have you noticed that strange object lying next to him? (She notices it for the first time) Could there be some connection between that object and his unusual condition? (She looks as though she is thinking very hard, trying to make sense of all this) What if you turned that switch, would it turn the device off and let him return to consciousness? (She seems to have an idea about the switch and begins turning it) *Don't touch* that switch! It might blow up. (She abruptly changes her mind about this tactic) Run and get help, *now!* (She bolts and runs out of the room).

Although withholding information from non-actors can sometimes be useful, one of the reasons for not doing so too often is the prime requisite that the actors participate as much as possible in the venture of making the film they are in. It is true that in a limited sense they are being used as photographic objects, but it is far truer that they are vitally involved in the creative process of making a film as good as possible. It is important that they understand why a shot is being repeated from a different angle or why they are being asked to do things that the film-maker suddenly contradicts, or where in the editing structure it is anticipated that a certain closeup reaction will be very useful. As you go along in the shooting you can help your actors achieve a sense of enthusiasm and energy by explaining to them the reasons for what you are doing. They need to be assured that you know what you are doing with them, and that what is being accomplished is worth their effort.

Since so much of what can be accomplished with non-actors depends on manipulation of their spontaneous reactions, it might be wondered how this affects the conduct of rehearsals. Since it would be disastrous to try to rehearse emotional reactions, these must be left out, and the rehearsals should concentrate only on the overall aspects of the action and dialogue. This allows the film-maker to check out how the camera angles and camera motions will actually work, and gives the actors a sense of their overall direction. The emotional intensity and shading should be striven for only during the actual shooting.

In documentary film-making, especially in the form know as *cinéma vérité,* there is no planning at all of what will happen. Documentary is very much akin to journalism, in which what actually happens is reported, ideally with no manipulation at all. In such filming the mechanics of making a film would ideally be invisible, so as not to intrude upon the natural course of events. The necessity for using such equipment as cameras, lights, microphones and sound recorders has an effect upon the situation that should be minimized by all means possible.

There are several methods of procedure which greatly minimize the intrusion of the film-maker into the situation he is trying to record. For one thing, the people being filmed are very curious about the strange equipment and what will be done with it. The sooner you can manage to get their curiosity satisfied, the sooner the situation will resume its natural course. It is often helpful to film for a while with an empty camera. This is especially effective with children, who will at first turn to stare at the camera every time they hear it running, or will drop whatever they are doing and stare into the lens. But since there is really very little for them to see, they quickly lose interest and accept the filming equipment matter-of-factly. Similar tactics apply to the use of lights—it is best to turn them all on as soon as they are set, and to leave them on during the entire shooting session. The usual economies of studio practice are best abandoned in the documentary situation, since the lights going off and on startle non-actors and abruptly reminds them that they are in a film. A camera that will run silently is very helpful, even if sync sound is not being shot. By resting a camera such as an Eclair on your shoulder and looking at all times only through the viewfinder, your subjects will have no way of knowing when you are shooting and when not, and thus you will intrude upon them minimally.

Of course it often happens in documentary filming that the factors necessary for good photography and sound recording will conflict with the necessity of allowing the true happenings to occur naturally. A technically polished film that has been achieved at the cost of losing the life of the content of the film must be considered a failure. On the other hand, a sloppy and ill-made film cannot be excused on the grounds that the procedures to make it technically better would have destroyed the content. The maxim that there is always some way to achieve technically acceptable results rarely fails, except where there is lack of ingenuity and care.

When film that has just been shot is sent to the laboratory for developing and work printing, the work print is usually refered to as the "rushes," simply because you are always in a rush to see them. If your film is shot over a period of time that allows rushes to be seen before all the shooting is completed, it is very productive to invite the people who appear in the film to the screening. In the case of a dramatic film, the actors will learn a great deal by seeing themselves on screen, and will be able to improve their performances. In the case of documentary films, it often happens that the people mainly in the film, since they know the scene they live in better than you do, will make very important suggestions when they see the rushes. They are apt to think of people and places and happenings which could be filmed to express the theme of the film more powerfully and with more inside savvy than you could do on your own.

Making a good film requires pulling a large number of different factors together into a cohesive presentation. The film-maker relies upon inventors, scientists and engineers to provide the machinery and materials with which films are made, and he should be as ready to seek out the resources of personality and mind and inspiration which can be found in the people who appear in his films. The film-maker is the focal point at which the contributions of all these people combine to form an image in the minds of the cinema audience.

17

ways of recording sound

The most difficult assignment in sound recording is getting clear, intelligible, dialogue recorded in synchronization with the actor's lip motions, especially when the film is being shot on location. We will use a section from an imaginary cowboy film to show the use of professional techniques and equipment for making good dialogue recordings under a variety of adverse conditions.

The most emphatic rule of procedure in dialogue sound recording is to get the microphone close to the speaker. This causes several good things to happen. Most important, the recording will have an acoustical characteristic known as "presence," which means that the voice of the speaker seems to be near the viewer's ears, out in the theater, and not stuffed back in a closet behind the screen. Another advantage of a close mike is that room reverberations and background noise are greatly minimized, since the mike, being closer to the speaker than to anything else, hears the voice far louder than the ambient noise.

The first scene of this cowboy film shows two men sitting close to their morning campfire, having a conversation. The soundman will want to put a mike right in close to them, but the cameraman does not want the mike to appear in the shot. This situation is one which must constantly be solved in film-making by a variety of methods. Since the actors are not going anywhere, the easiest solution is to place the mike right in front of the actors, but hiding it behind something in the scene so that it will not be noticed. It could be set on a little swivel stuck right in the ground but hidden from the camera view by the battered old coffeepot. The mike cable can easily be covered over with a little earth and run to a conveniently placed recording machine out of sight.

The choice of microphone type for this shot would be a general-purpose directional mike, which gives extra presence to sounds in a straight line in front of it, but is very unresponsive to sounds from any other direction. Use of this mike would be feasible only if the two men were sitting close together, so that they were both on the axis of the mike's pickup pattern. If they were sitting on opposite sides of the fire, left and right, then an omnidirectional mike might be used; this picks up sounds coming from an area consisting of a half-sphere in front of it. This type of mike gains this advantage at the sacrifice of some amount of presence and background-noise rejection, but in this case, where the actors are quite close to the mike, and there is very little background noise or reverberation, an omnidirectional mike would be a good choice.

In the next shot the men get up and walk over to their horses, all the while carrying on a conversation which must be recorded clearly. The usual solution here is to suspend the mike out over the actor's heads, on the end of an aluminum pole. The pole is manipulated by a man standing to one side of the camera frame of view, so that the mike moves along with the men just a few feet above their heads. This shot will require a little rehearsal so that the mike will not accidentally bob down into camera view as the soundman moves it to follow the men. Another solution to this situation is one commonly used in documentary filming where no rehearsal is possible, since events are filmed as they happen. A special type of microphone is used, which includes in its design an acoustical tube a foot or two long and about the diameter of a garden hose; this gathers sound from a very narrow angle in front of it and makes it more present, even though the person talking may be ten feet away. This mike, called a shotgun mike because of its appearance, carries the characteristics of the directional mike to an extreme. It does not produce sound of as good quality at close range as a standard mike does, and so should not be used except as a special-purpose problem solver. A soundman using this mike would simply hold it in his hand, aiming it very accurately at whoever was speaking and staying as close to them as he dared without getting into the view of the camera. An experienced soundman of this type achieves the ability to estimate fairly accurately the field of view of the camera by glancing at the position of the zoom lens control to see how far it is toward full telephoto or wide angle.

In the next shot, the men are galloping along on their horses, and the camera is trucking alongside them in a pickup truck, which also contains the soundman with his mike out on the end of the pole. It is important that the soundman be wearing a pair of earphones plugged into the recording machine so that he can hear the sound exactly as it is being picked up by the mike. In this example, what he hears is a horrible crashing, an intermittent thudding sound, caused by the wind hitting the microphone. This problem is frequently encountered when recording in a windy location, even when the mike isn't moving along at thirty miles an hour. It is solved by using a windscreen, usually made of spun plastic, which fits over the mike and acts as a pillow against the wind, but does not degrade the quality of the voices.

By now the men are crossing the desert, and a fierce sandstorm has come up, howling at 60 mph and filling the air with so much sand it is hard to see. The wind is being made by airplane propellers driven by gasoline engines. In this tremendous roar it is impossible to record dialogue with acceptable quality, even with the best of special equipment, so the scenes are filmed silently, with the men speaking their lines for the camera only. Later, in the studio, they will watch their images on the screen and speak their lines to match their photographed lip movements. This will be recorded and mixed with a wind-sound effect, yielding an effective and understandable sound track.

The men finally make it to town and head for the saloon to drink some whiskey. There is a wide-angle shot in which the two men are at the bar, standing in profile right up close to the camera, and suddenly, on the balcony in the background, appears a mean-looking hombre who says coolly that he told them to stay out of town. One of the cowboys replies that they got thirsty. The mean hombre pulls out his Colt and shoots the glass out of the fellow's hand.

In this sequence the mean hombre and the men at the bar are separated by about thirty feet, so they will each require a mike of their own. Getting good presence on the hombre on the balcony might be difficult with a mike outside the camera frame of view, so a tiny mike called a lavalier mike could be hung around his neck and concealed behind his kerchief. Its cable could easily be hidden behind the balcony railing. The cables coming from the two mikes will both need to be run into a small box having volume-control knobs, called a mixer. This enables the sound levels from the two mikes to be adjusted to whatever relative levels are desired. The mixer output is then fed into the recording machine. Mixers commonly have four or five separate inputs, allowing that many mikes to be used at once.

The blast of noise that the gun makes is so loud in comparison to the speakers' voices that it will completely overload the recording machine and the gunshot sound will be unsatisfactory. There are various solutions, but the surest one is to discard the blast recorded at the time of the filming and insert a specially made gunshot-sound effect into the track at exactly the right point.

We have been carefully considering microphone usage in the scenes described, but ignoring the requirements for camera and sound recorder. The most important requirement is that there be some way of ultimately combining the picture and its corresponding sound together in perfect synchronization. The most sophisticated and most convenient method requires a camera which has been adapted to run at *exactly* 24 fps. This is done by using a small transistor circuit containing a crystal oscillator that pulses at precisely a fixed frequency. This provides a timing standard which is amplified and used to control the running speed of the camera's motor.

The most convenient and flexible

sound recorder to use on location is the Nagra ¼-inch tape recorder. This machine can also be fitted with an oscillator identical to the unit used to control the camera speed. The output of this oscillator does not control the tape running speed. It is recorded along the edge of the sound tape, and thus provides a precise timing reference along with sound, which can be used later to synchronize picture to sound.

Shooting synchronous sound and picture by this method works because both picture and sound are referred to an exact timing standard provided by the oscillators in the two machines operating at exactly the same frequency. The advantage of this system over the conventional method is that there is no mechanical or electrical connection between the camera and recorder, thus allowing them to be used with complete physical independence of each other.

The more commonly used method of sychronization is a variation of the above method. The camera is equipped with an internal sync pulse generator which is a part of its motor. The output frequency of this generator is exactly proportional to the running speed of the camera. This output is fed through a wire into the tape recorder, where it is recorded along the edge of the sound track, as before. This means that the sound recording now contains not only the sound, but also an exact record of the camera running speed at any point along the track. This record is used at a later stage to synchronize the picture and sound. The main operating difference between this method and the first is that in this method the camera and recorder are tied together by a wire, which under some circumstances seriously inhibits the physical freedom of the cameraman and soundman.

The Nagra tape recorder is about the size of a Manhattan telephone book, and so it can be carried around easily. In documentary film-making, the soundman carries it by a strap over the shoulder, leaving his hands free to climb around with the microphone. He is thus free to move around to whatever position is advantageous and to walk along following the action. The camera, most likely an Elair, Arriflex, or converted Auricon, can also be carried around on the shoulder. With these, an extremely quick and flexible sync sound shooting crew can be made up of only two men.

When a sync sound film is being edited, each of the camera takes will have to be lined up side by side in sync with its corresponding sound track. Doing this without some sort of start mark on both the picture and sound would take an inordinate amount of time, so start marks must be made at the time of shooting. The most traditional way of doing this is to have the camera and recorder start rolling; then a small slate with the scene number on it is put into the camera field of view. On the top of the slate is mounted a piece of wood about a foot long, hinged to the slate at one end. The person holding the slate reads aloud the information written on it, then slaps the top board down on the top of the slate, making a bang. The editor can later line up the bang on the sound track with the picture frame in which the board has just hit the top of the slate. The sound and picture can then be run in sync (more about this in Chapter 18). Some cameras have a built-in start mark device consisting of a tiny light that flashes inside the camera, exposing a single frame, and at the same time sends a beep tone over the sync pulse wire into the tape recorder. This is called an automatic clapper. The flash frame and beep can later be used as start marks. In lieu of a clapboard, or in case of a failure of the automatic beep system, one of the actors can simply clap his hands together at the beginning or end of the shot. In documentary shooting it is sometimes common to rush into shooting a fast-breaking action, and not put start marks or slate the scene until the end of the shot. This is not quite as convenient for the editor, but it works just as well.

Sometimes a sound-recording situation will arise in which radio microphones are a great help. Suppose a scene is to be shot in sync sound of a couple walking along a crowded sidewalk, having an important conversation. All the rest of the people in the shot are ordinary citizens who, we hope, will look natural. Even if we could track along with the couple using a mike on a pole, without hitting a No Parking sign or a store awning, the odd sight of the soundman and boom would disrupt the scene. Instead the actors can each be equipped with a tiny microphone, hidden in their clothing near their throats, which is capable of broadcasting the sound it picks up over an FM radio wave, and this can be monitored by a receiver at some distance and recorded. Such radio mike systems are made by Sennheiser and Comrex, among others. These systems are a further advance in getting rid of the wires connecting the various functions in sync sound shooting.

As an economy measure in shooting this scene, we could fall back on the old versatile technique of hiding the mike in the scene. Two assistants could be used, one to carry the tape recorder as though it were a brief-case, at the same time discreetly holding the microphone behind his back as he walked along directly in front of the actors. The second assistant could walk along between the mike and the camera, screening it from view. A directional mike, such as an Electrovoice 666, would be a good choice for this scene, since it could favor the actors' voices over the street noises. The assistant who carried it behind his back must aim it directly at the actors' mouths.

When shooting sync sound it is usually necessary to use a camera that does not make any noise, or the sound recordings will be marred by camera chatter. Some cameras are nearly noiseless, and others must be mounted inside an accessory sound-proofing blimp in order to be used as sound cameras. The noiseless cameras, especially in 16mm, are much easier to use. Examples are the Eclair, Mitchell BNC, Arriflex and Auricon cameras mentioned before. For the sake of convenience and economy, many scenes requiring sync sound can be shot with non-silent cameras. In the example of the sidewalk conversation, the camera would probably be mounted inside a station wagon in order to track it along with the actors, and this insulation, combined with the sound-masking effect of the street hubbub, would make a silent camera unnecessary.

Another way of avoiding camera noise is to use a directional mike up close to the actors and then have the camera placed some distance away, using a telephoto lens to get closer shots. This is an expedient technique and often used. If just a little camera chatter still comes through (perhaps when shooting in a quiet room), then a heavy blanket draped over the camera and the cameraman will solve the problem. If all else fails, there is still the last-ditch technique of masking remaining camera noise later during the sound mix by adding the sound effect of traffic, or an air conditioner, or a shower running.

Shooting film which does not require sync sound simplifies things greatly. A noisy camera may be used, it does not have to run at exact speed, it can be moved around without danger of including the mike in the shot, shots do not have to be slated, and the camerman is free to follow his eyes. When recording the sound, the microphone can be placed where it will work best without worrying about messing up a shot, the recorder can be simpler and less expensive, less expensive mikes can usually be used because of the freedom of mike placement, and the soundman is free to follow his ears. It should be noted that a great amount of filming is not sync sound. Even theatrical features often consist of hardly more than 50 per cent sync sound. The impression of sync sound running all the way through a film is created by a scattering of it intermittently throughout the length of the film. A great deal of time is taken up with action, gestures, scenic long shots, fights, and significant looks between actors.

The good-quality tape recorders made for home use by such companies as Ampex, Sony, Uher, Panasonic, Concord and Wollensak are capable of sound quality entirely suitable for film use, when sync dialogue is not being recorded. The microphones supplied with these machines are usually not anywhere near as good as the machines, and are of such poor acoustical design that they do not record words well beyond a distance of two or three feet. One of the better microphones made by Shure or Electrovoice in the $50 to $70 price range will work much better.

Recording tape is inexpensive in comparison to other materials used making a film, so the best should always be used. Typical of the several good brands is Scotch, type 201, which is designed to have a very low background noise level and is silicone-lubricated to reduce friction and wear of the heads on the recorder. Experience has shown that it is usually best not to record on extended-play tape because its thinner base stretches and causes timing variations, makes editing the tape physically more difficult and tends to print through sounds from one turn of tape on the reel to the next.

When transferring sound from one recording to another, it is best not to use the microphone but to make an electrical connection from the sound source to the recording machine. For example, if you want to transfer some music from a record onto a tape machine, you could just play the record and put the tape recorder mike next to the record-player speaker. However, the sound quality will be much better if you connect either the record player pre-amp or speaker terminals into the line or aux input on the tape recorder, thus recording directly by wire.

The standard running speed for tape machines in motion-picture work is 7½ inches per second. Running at a slower speed sacrifices some high-frequency response, makes precise cutting of the tape more difficult, and is incompatible with most of the tape machines at the sound labs. Recording a sound at 7½ ips and playing it back at 3¾ ips results in the sounds lasting twice as long and in lowering the pitch by one octave. There are often good reasons for doing this, particularly when creating sound effects. Sounds such as wind, breathing, laughter, screams, engines and drumming take on a different character at half speed. Since these sounds will have to be cut into the tape sound track, which will be running at the standard speed of 7½ ips, you will need to make a dub of the effect at that speed. The procedure is to record the sound you want at 7½ ips but then play it back at 3¾ ips, copying it onto another machine running at 7½ ips. This gives a recording of the special effect, which can be spliced into the sound track. Sounds may also be more effective when doubled in speed. The desired sound is recorded at 3¾ ips, and then spliced directly into the rest of the soundtrack, which will be played at 7½ ips.

There is a difficulty in using home-type tape recorders for film use because the standard track width of the professional recording and playback machines is nearly the full width of the ¼-inch tape. If you submit a sound track made on a half-track or quarter-track machine to the lab for transfer in the process of making sound prints of the film, their machine will pick up whatever is on the full width of the tape. This could be a disaster if there was some other recording on the other tracks that you did not know about. Even if those other tracks are clean, they still may contain residual tape noise, which will be picked up and become part of your sound track. There are full-track replacement heads available for most machines, and for professional work they should be used.

Sound effects are easily recorded out in the field with a battery-powered machine and a good microphone. But sometimes sounds are not readily available for recording by the film-maker, and it is fortunate that sound-effects records, offering a huge variety of sounds both familiar and bizarre, are plentiful, at about the same cost as music records. Jet-plane take-offs, ocean-liner horns, space-control-center talk, huge crowds cheering, elephants trumpeting, circus barkers, jackhammers, machine guns firing, and strange electronic sounds are all available on sound-effect records. In most cases these sounds may be used, even in commercial films, without any legal complications. However, if music from a commercial recording is used in a *commercial* film, it might lead to a copyright suit. In cases where the film is not used commercially, it is doubtful that there would be any difficulty over transfer of commercial records. When music is to be used in a commercial film it can be purchased from record companies, which maintain large collections of records that they sell outright, also charging a reasonable licensing fee for their commercial use.

Recording musical groups live, without a recording studio, is very tricky, but it can be done with acceptable results. If it is an unamplified group, and very small, an omnidirectional mike can be placed close to the floor and the group arranged in a circle around it. Make a test recording and see what imbalances there are in the instruments. Then move those that are too loud farther out in the circle. Record in the plushiest, most padded, drapery-laden, carpeted room you can find, so that there will be a minimum of room reverberation, and the end result will be pretty good. If the budget allows, use more than one mike and run them into a mixer, so that the sound balance from each can be adjusted to taste. When recording an electric group, it is best to separate the speakers for each instrument as much as possible and to use directional mikes in front of each speaker. The musicians will have to play not too loud in order to avoid overloading the mikes. Balance between the instruments can be effected either by the mixer controls on the mikes or by the amplifier controls on the instruments.

18

editing sound and picture

Now that we have finished gathering the pictures and sounds for a film, it's time to begin to put them all together in an effective form. It will be necessary first to explain about magnetic film. Trying to edit sprocketed film along with unsprocketed 1/4-inch sound tape would impose intolerable difficulties. The solution lies in the use of sprocketed magnetic film, which is either 16 mms or 35 mms wide, and identical to the picture film except that it is coated with a magnetic oxide like that on the recording tape. The sync-sound 1/4-inch tape is fed into a machine called a resolver, which plays the tape and makes a copy of it onto magnetic film. The speed at which the tape is run through the resolver is based on the sync-pulse signals recorded along the edge. Thus, if the camera slowed down during the filming, the sync-pulse signals would also have slowed down, and the resolver will slow the playback of the tape down by exactly the same amount. What we end up with on the magnetic film is a sound track which is in frame-for-frame correspondence with the picture. The picture and sound are now both on identical physical mediums, in frame-to-frame synchronization, and ready for editing.

The machine universally used for editing sync sound (in the United States) is the Moviola, made by the company of that name. The Moviola consists basically of a picture-viewing head and a magnetic film sound playback head, linked together mechanically so that they run in step, and a speed-control pedal that allows the material to run through at rates varying from a few frames per second to about 50 frames per second. The machine may also be stopped on any single frame and run backward at varying rates.

The picture roll of a scene is threaded up so that the start frame is exactly in the film gate in the picture head. The mag film is then threaded up so that the beep-tone start mark is exactly under the pick-up head. The picture head and sound head drive are then locked together by a simple slip collar, and the sound amplifier and picture lamp are then turned on. Pressing the foot pedal will cause the picture and sound to be presented in synchronism, going faster as the foot control is pressed down farther. If it is desired that they be displayed at the standard 24 fps projection speed, a switch is flipped that overrides the foot pedal and runs at this speed. The scene may be run backward and forward, slowed down, speeded up and stopped, until it is decided how it is to be cut.

We will imagine that the sequence to be edited is a conversation between a couple, and that the first shot we are looking at is the girl speaking. This shot is run on the Moviola until we get to the point where we want to cut to the man's face and his line of dialogue. Use a grease pencil or other suitable marker to mark both the picture frame and sound frame where the cut is to occur. The picture head and sound head on the Moviola are hinged so that you can

A 35mm Moviola editing machine. Note the slide coupling just above the speaker circle. This connects or disconnects the picture head on the right from the sound head on the left. *(Courtesy F&B/Ceco, Inc.*

Picture and magnetic sound lined up in sync on a 16mm Moviola. (*Machine courtesy Ross-Gaffney, Inc.*

swing them out of the way for doing this. The material can then be lifted out of the machine and cut with a scissors.

(Be sure to cut through the frame *after* the last frame of picture you want to keep, to allow for what will be trimmed off by either the tape or cement splicer.)

The picture and sound rolls of the man can now be threaded up with their start marks in the right places. Run this material until you are just at the point where you want his action to begin. Mark the picture frame immediately preceding the first frame you want, and do likewise with the sound track. Lift these out and cut them as before. The beginning of the shot of the man can now be spliced to the end of the shot of girl, and the beginning of his sound track can be spliced to the end of her sound (splicing techniques are discussed at the end of Chapter 10). You can now view this sequence of two scenes by threading up the spliced picture and sound rolls with their beginning start marks. The girl will appear on the screen and speak, and at the point you picked to cut, the man will appear and speak in return. Synchronism is maintained because once a picture and corresponding sound roll have been locked into the Moviola in sync, according to their start marks, they are run in sync by the machine all through their length. The start marks for picture and sound at the very beginning of the film are all that need be retained.

With a little more finesse, we can now do some more interesting kinds of cutting. These include cutting away from a person speaking to a reaction shot of the person being spoken to, and then cutting back to the first person just as he is finishing his speech. Keeping all of this in sync is not difficult if it is done with a method clearly in mind. In this case we will start again with the girl talking. At a key point she is in the midst of saying something that we know will surprise the man very much. Just at this point, the audience will want to see his surprise but to continue to hear what she is saying. In editing this, we will want to cut the picture of her, but not her sound track, which will be continued on to the end of her speech. In order to maintain sync, all that is necessary is to make sure that for whatever length of her shot we cut out we add *exactly* that length of shot of the man's surprise. In other words, if we want to put in 80 frames of the man's surprise, we must take 80 frames out of the middle of the shot of the girl talking. Since we will be *taking out* 80 frames of her shot and *adding* 80 frames of his shot, we have not broken sync.

The first thing to do in actually accomplishing this is to look at the man's reaction shot. (Woe if you have not got one.) Choose what part of that shot you want, cut it out and keep it handy. Let's assume it is exactly 80 frames long. Now thread up the shot of the girl talking, and her corresponding sound track side by side in sync in the Moviola. Run through the shot until you get to the point in her dialogue where the audience will be in suspense to see how he is reacting. Stop the machine right there and mark the frame following the last frame of the girl you want to keep. Also mark the corresponding frame of the sound track, for future reference. Take the shot of her out of the Moviola and place it in a synchronizer (see picture), which will measure the number of frames you run through it. To do this, set the marked frame on the 1 of the frame counter wheel and roll through the scene until you have measured off 80 frames. On the 80th frame (actually above the number 40 on the wheel after two revolutions), make a mark. You can now cut the marked 80-frame section out of her shot and splice in the 80-frame section of his shot. To view your handiwork, place the spliced sequence into the Moviola with the first frame of the cutaway shot of the man in the film gate. This will be in line with the mark you made before on the sound track. Run the machine backward to the start of the sequence, and now you can run the sequence and see how well it works.

In the manner described above, you may freely intercut sync-sound footage with all sorts of detail shots that were shot silent. For example,

The numbered wheel on the front of the synchronizer can be used to count frames as the film rolls through to the right. *(Machine courtesy Ross-Gaffney, Inc.)*

at appropriate points you might cut away to someone looking in the window, or to a closeup of the girl nervously tapping the ash off her cigarette, or even to images that relate to the specific things she is saying.

It is a common practice, though not absolutely necessary, to have code numbers printed in yellow ink along the edges of the mag sound track and the picture. These numbers begin at the start marks and progress by one digit, appearing usually every foot along the edge. Thus you have, in effect, sync marks on picture and sound every foot of the way. Any time you need sync reference you merely line up, for example, code number 103 on the picture with 103 on the sound. This can save a lot of editing time on long films containing a great deal of sync footage.

When the dialogue and picture are all cut, the dialogue track can be put aside, and the sound effects, which have also been recorded on mag film, can be set into place. Horses galloping, engines running, tires squealing, gunshots, crowd noises, and so on, are placed in the Moviola alongside their corresponding picture. The places on the sound track between sound effects are filled in with blank mag film. Sound effects that run continuously through a sequence and are not required to synchronize with anything in the picture can be started right at the first frame of sequence and run through to the last, even though they be desired only occasionally during the sequence. An example of this would be an eerie electronic sound representing the menacing presence of a strange giant creature. In the finished film it is desired that this sound fade in just before the creature appears and fade

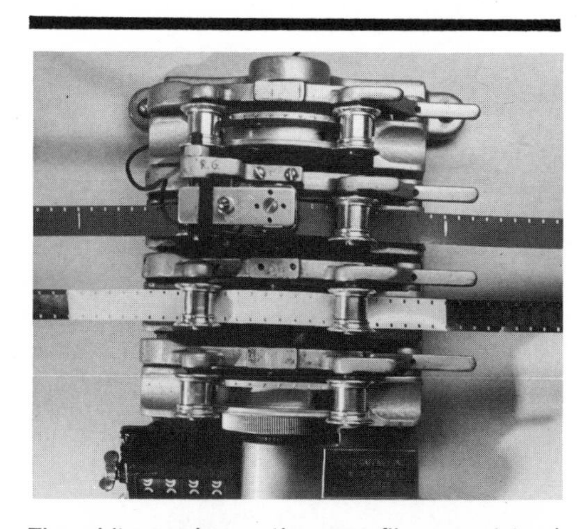

The white marks on the mag film sound track indicate where a cutaway from the speaker on the picture roll was desired. The cutaway from the speaker is represented (for illustration only) by the white leader.

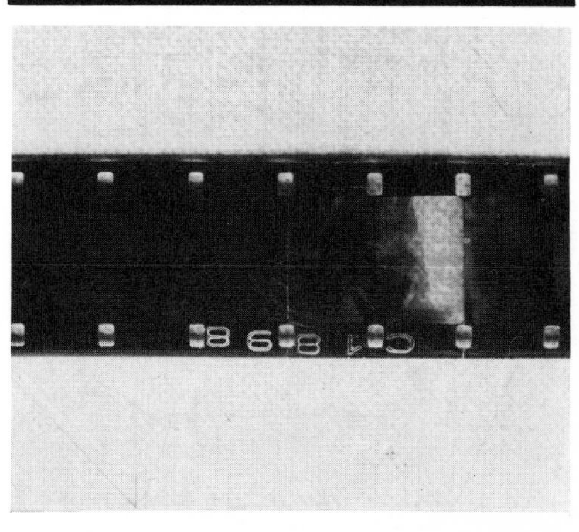

Inked edge numbers.

out as it recedes. There may be numerous places in the sequence where this sound effect will be used, and rather than try to prepare pieces of the effect, complete with fades in and out for each of the occasions it will be used, it is much simpler to have the effect continuously available on the effects track, and to fade it in and out with a volume control during the re-recording mix, which combines all the tracks together (see Chapter 19).

This is also true of the music track, which in the finished film will come on strong at times, fade completely out at others, and just simmer in the background at others. All this control can be more easily accomplished during the mix, and what is required at the editing stage is that the music is synced up with the scenes for which it will be used. To what degree and to what loudness that music will ultimately be used is determined at the mixing session.

The total number of tracks prepared for a film depends entirely on the needs of the particular film. We have outlined the basic three: dialogue, sound effects and music. In complex films there may be several more tracks of sound effects and music. Whenever more than one sound effect is to be heard at the same time, it is customary to have those sounds on separate tracks so that they can be combined at will. Whenever one piece of music is to blend with or dissolve into another, then the second piece of music will have to be on a separate track.

It is possible to get around the need for a Moviola by using the synchronizer in conjunction with a mag sound head and a picture viewer (see pictures). The most convenient way of using this setup is to put the synchronizer just to the right of the picture viewer, and line both up so that the picture strip goes through the viewer and then through one of the rear gangs (roller sections) of the synchronizer. The mag sound is placed in the front gang, on which is mounted the mag reader head. Just as in using the Moviola, the start mark for the sound is placed directly under the pickup head, and the start mark for the picture is placed in the film gate of the viewer. The mag sound head is connected to an amplifier and speaker. The reels of picture and sound are pulled through by the rewinds, which are equipped with slip clutches so that the picture and sound will wind up evenly. As the rewind on the right is turned, the picture and sound will be pulled through the synchronizer exactly in synchronization, and picture and corresponding sound will be presented. The disadvantage of this setup compared to the Moviola is that it is very tricky to wind the material through the system at an even speed. (However, a small drive motor for the synchronizer is available as an accessory.) It is more likely that a mistake in maintaining sync will be made, since this method depends on the distance between the viewer and synchronizer's remaining absolutely the same, and on the film between the viewer and synchronizer's remaining taut. It is possible to put up with drawbacks and get satisfactory results—and the elimination of the need for a costly, heavy Moviola is a considerable advantage for the no-budget filmmaker.

In making a film, in which only a few sync points occur in its entire length, there is a procedure that eliminates the need for mag film and a

The magnetic pickup head rides on the mag film as it passes through the synchronizer.

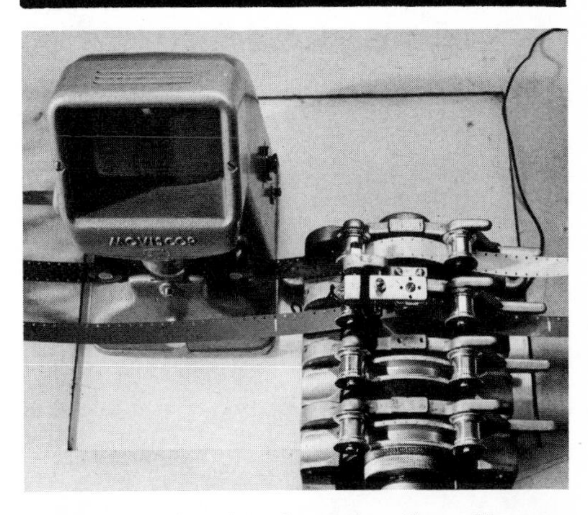

Using a synchronizer in conjunction with magnetic pickup head and picture viewer as a substitute for a Moviola. Picture and sound are pulled through in frame-for-frame sync by the synchronizer.

The spring loaded slip clutch on the rewind shaft allows picture and sound reels to be wound evenly.

A positive optical sound track.

sound reader entirely. Suppose this film requires that the music change to another sound exactly at a certain point in the film. The film is set up on the rewinds and run, from the beginning, through the synchronizer, until the exact changeover point is reached. The footage counter on the synchronizer reads, let's say, 360 feet. This is converted by arithmetic to the equivalent time of exactly ten minutes, if the film is in 16mm. You then cut the sound track, which is on ¼-inch tape, so that when played on the tape recorder, the changeover occurs ten minutes after the beginning of the track. The tape is then taken to the lab where a copy of it is made in the form of an optical track. This is a photographic version of the sound, printed along one edge of a clear piece of 16mm film (see picture). Regardless of what previous synchronizing and editing procedure has been used, the sound track will ultimately be transferred into an optical anyway, so this does not represent an extra step required by the short-cut method being described. Since the sound is now on sprocketed material recorded at 24 fps, it is the equivalent of a mag track, in terms of timing. This optical track can be played on a sound projector, and the changeover point in the sound identified and marked (be sure not to mark on the track area itself). The mark can be lined up in the synchronizer with the cut point in the picture material, then run backwards through the synchronizer to the beginning, and start marks can then be placed on the front of picture and sound rolls. When the picture and sound are printed together to make a finished film, the music will change right on cue.

If brief passages of sync-sound dialogue are desired in a film, and shooting it synchronously is out of the question, there is a way it may be accomplished. The dialogue is recorded on ¼-inch tape, with the actors going through as many as possible of the physical motions and postures that will be filmed. When the shots are made in which the actors are to speak, the camera is adjusted carefully to run at 24 fps, or a sync motor is used, and while the tape recorder plays back the actor's voices, they mimic their own voices. This will give a picture and sound track that are very close together in terms of sync. Minor adjustments can be made after the ¼-inch tape is transfered onto mag film. Since sound is not being recorded during the filming, a noisy camera may be used. Once the dialogue is on the mag film, it can be edited synchronously with the picture, as described already. This technique is used extensively in theatrical musical films, where it would otherwise be impossible to cut from shot to shot during a musical number, and still have the music continue smoothly in synchronism with the performers.

In a situation like the example given in Chapter 16 in which the dialogue could not be recorded during a windstorm, the picture sequence is edited first. Then it is projected by a sync projector (24 fps exactly) and mimicked by the actors. Their voices are recorded on a sync mag film recorder. Picture and sound can then be edited as though they had been filmed synchronously.

In these two procedures, which simulate sync-sound shooting, the first involves recording the *sound* first, and then shooting picture with lip motions to match it. The second procedure shoots the *picture* first, and then records sounds to match it. Either method demands considerable skill and practice by the actors. But either method can also solve horrendous problems and save a lot of money.

Instead of doing all the sound editing on mag film, it can sometimes be done, all or in part, on ¼-inch tape, as a means of getting around the considerable cost involved in mixing magnetic film tracks. We will make a sound track for a hypothetical film which does not require sync dialogue but which does need music in several places, some sound effects, and voices speaking about what is seen on the screen. Let's start with the voices.

We have recorded interviews, expressing their feelings about the subject, with people who appear in the film. Culling all the best remarks out of the recordings, we now want to

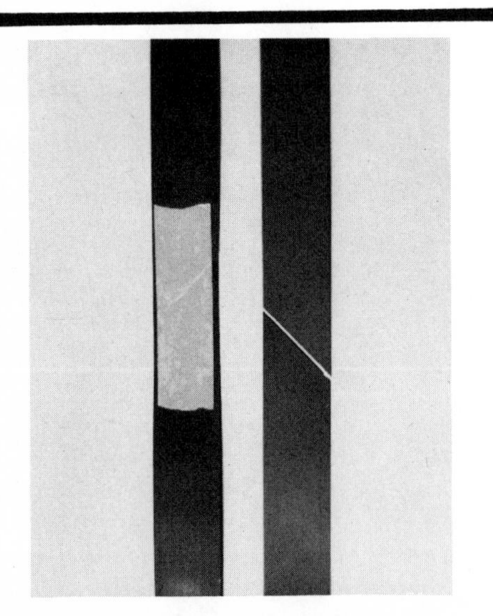

A spliced piece of ¼-inch recording tape.

By running the tape to the left of the drive capstan, instead of between the capstan and the rubber roller, the tape will not be pulled through the tape recorder.

splice them together into a coherent commentary. Tape is spliced by making a diagonal cut across the ends of the pieces to be joined and then placing a strip of splicing tape over the cut to be joined, on the back (shiny side) of the tape (see picture). The design of the diagonal cut sliding over the recording and playback head of the tape machine is such that there is no discernible disturbance heard as the splice goes by. There will be no difficulty in finding exactly the point at which to cut the tape if you are merely lifting out whole sentences and phrases. In normal speech patterns there are pauses between phrases of about 1/4 second to a full second. Since the tape is running at 7 1/2 inches per second, there will be between two and seven inches of blank space between the sections of speech, and so cutting between them is not difficult. In many cases, however, there may be no pause between words at a point where you wish to cut, and in this case an error of only 1/4 inch, insignificant before, will clip off the first or last letter of a word. In order to solve this, lift the tape from its normal position between the pinch roller and the drive capstan (see picture). When you turn the tape machine to forward, the tape will not be pulled through. You are now free to move the tape over the playback manually by turning the reels with your fingers. Turning slowly, you will be able to hear each syllable of each word (at a much lower pitch, of course), and by rocking the tape forward and backward across the pickup head you can find exactly where one syllable of a word ends and the next begins. Mark the tape with a felt pen at the exact center of the pickup head, lift the tape out and cut it for splicing.

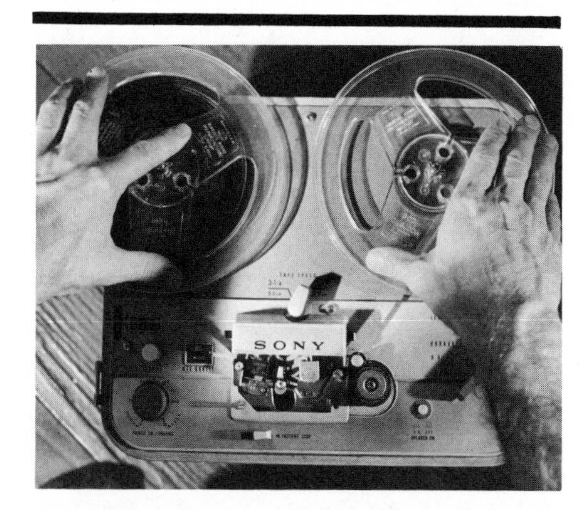

The tape can now be passed manually back and forth over the playback head for precise location of sounds.

The X marks the spot where the signal on the tape is being picked up by the playback head.

When the voice tape is all assembled you are ready to make the music and sound-effects tape. Splice together all the music you will need, recorded at full volume, and cut in time lengths to match the time lengths of the picture with which they will be used. Let's assume a sequence where no music will be used, but you will want a sound effect of busy traffic. Since the part of the music track corresponding to that sequence would have contained blank tape, you might save making a separate sound track by splicing the traffic sound into that blank space. You now have a voice track and a music-and-effects track, which are cut to the timing of the picture, and you are ready to mix them together (see next chapter), preparatory to having a sound print made of the film. Before mixing them, it is best to run each, one at a time, while the picture is being projected. Ideally, the projector would run at exactly 24 fps, so that picture and sound will be presented in approximate sync. The older Bell and Howell 16mm projectors are adjustable to within fairly accurate limits. The running speed can be checked by measuring a minute's worth of film out on the synchronizer and punching a hole in the first and last frame. Run this through the projector and time it with a watch to see if it takes exactly 60 seconds. To adjust the running speed of the projector, take it out of the enclosure and remove the cover over the back of the drive motor (see picture). There is a pair of contact points that spin when the motor runs. By adjusting the two screws that set the tension on the points, the running speed may be altered. By adjusting the contact points close together the motor will

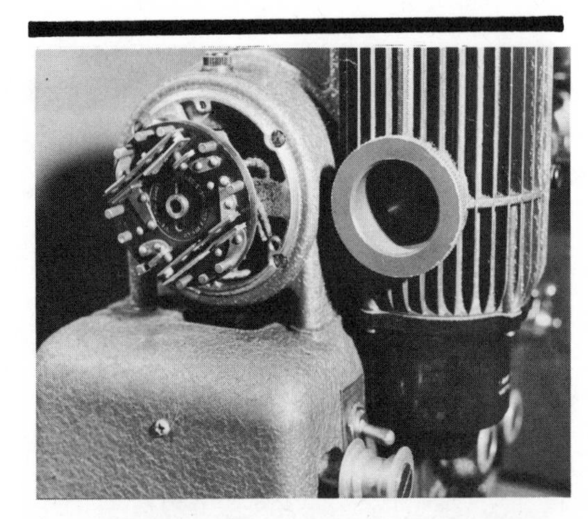

A Bell & Howell projector with the rear motor cover removed. There are two set screws which adjust the contact points, all of which spin as the motor runs.

be speeded up, and setting the points farther apart will slow it down.

In editing magnetic film, a splicer that makes diagonal cuts is used, for the same reason that magnetic tape is cut that way. Plastic tape with perforations in it is used to join the pieces together (see picture).

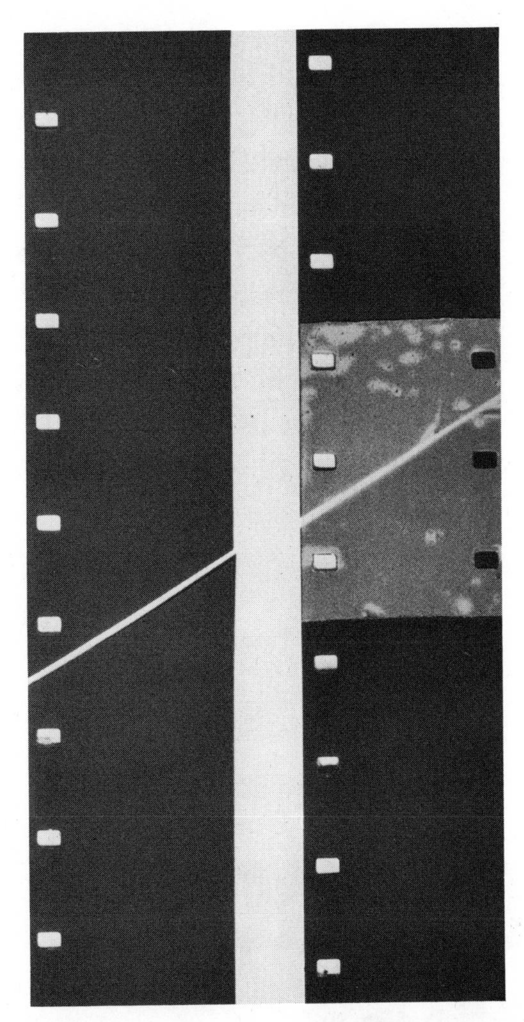

A splice in magnetic film, made with perforated tape.

Two models of the Siemens 16mm interlock projector. This unique machine will record sound on magnetic film and will play it back in frame-for-frame sync with the picture being projected from the opposite side of the machine. *(Courtesy Arriflex Corporation, Inc.)*

19

mixing sounds together

The purpose of a mixing session is to combine the contents of all the sound tracks together, in the proportions and loudnesses desired, and re-record all of this on a single strand of magnetic film. Studios equipped to do such work are available for hire and are a necessity when the sound tracks are synchronous and complex. Mixing studios generally have facilities arranged in the following manner: There is a whole set of magnetic-film playback machines to accommodate a large number of separate sound tracks. Each of these playback decks is fed into a master control panel, which provides a volume control, and very capable tone-contour controls, for each of the sound tracks. In addition there are usually connections available into echo chambers, reverberation units and tape echo devices, so that sounds on the mag-film tracks can be modified as they are re-recorded in the mix.

All of the playback decks, the projector and the re-recording machine are electrically connected by a system known as interlock, which means that they all run exactly in step, frame for frame. For example, if the projector were stopped and run backward 100 frames, all the mag-film machines would stop with it and together back up 100 frames.

The projector is usually in a soundproof room at the rear of the projection room (as in a regular movie theater), so that its clatter does not disturb the sound work. An electric clock that tells time by dropping numerals into place is often projected onto the screen at one corner so that the mixer can be cued as to when scenes are about to begin and end.

With some knowledge of the physical facilities, we will be able to watch a mix going on and understand what is being done. The room goes dark. The faint whir of machinery is heard starting up. On the screen a large white circle appears for one frame, and at the same instant a loud beep is heard. The circle is actually a start-mark hole punched into the picture leader. The beep is the composite sound of all the start-mark beeps on the three sound tracks being mixed. Since all the beeps and the appearance of circle occurred at the same instant, we can be assured that all the material for the mix is now running in sync.

On the screen appears a lonely deserted beach. At the same time, the mixer turns up the volume controls on tracks 2 and 3, so that the sound of surf (track 2) and a mournful foghorn (track 3) are faded in smoothly and mixed together. Up to this time track 1 has not been used, but of course it has been running along in frame-for-frame sync all this time. It contains narration, which is about to begin, according to the time-cue sheet that the mixer is keeping an eye on, so he turns up the volume on track 1. A man's voice is heard saying, "My wife and I often walked on the beach"—we can now see their figures appearing at a distant through the light fog—"so this seemed like any other foggy morning at first." The couple on the screen have approached much closer now, and we can see that they are talking together. The mixer had turned down the volume control on track 1 immediately after the end of the man's voice, because track 1 next carries the sync sound of the couple's talking. The mixer slowly turns up the volume on track 1, and we begin to hear what the couple is saying as they get closer. They are talking about the role beaches have played in animal evolution. As they come up into a full-frame closeup, the wife suddenly exclaims, "Look!" In an even larger closeup, the man's head lifts up suddenly to look, and his eyes are very big (this shot lasts only 24 frames). There on the beach, right in front of them, is a huge whale. *Whannnng!* goes a sudden sharp chord of "shock" music, right at the instant of the cut to the whale (this was on track 3, between blasts of the foghorn). The couple are now chattering excitedly about this discovery, in medium closeup. The shot then cuts to looking over their shoulders so that we can get another good look at the whale. At present, track 1 is carrying their voices, track 2 is still carrying the surf sound, and track 3, having delivered the burst of music, has reverted to carrying the foghorn, which was very atmospheric at first, but is now getting in the way and intruding on the dialogue and the story, so the mixer is carefully fading it out. The couple are then seen in medium closeup, moving toward the whale for a closer look. They are talking about what could have caused it to be on the beach, and in the midst of their conversation a loud voice demands, "Who are you?" This voice overlaps the dialogue of the couple, so it could not be carried by track 1. Track 2 is running surf, but track 3 has just become available because it has finished with the foghorn. The strange voice, where it overlaps with the sync dialogue, is on track 3. The shot cuts to a man striding out of the open mouth of the whale. Then a medium closeup of the startled couple, standing frozen in their tracks. A conversation begins, all on track 1, in which the stranger tells them that his fishing skiff was rammed by this whale, and that he found himself scooped up inside it. But once inside he found it was the interior of an ultramodern submarine, with nobody aboard. The couple want to come inside to see this. Track 2, which has been carrying surf sound, is faded out, so that the eerie, anticipatory music that comes next on this track can be faded in as the couple start to go inside the whale-submarine. Track 3, which has been blank since the strange voice interrupted with "Who are you?" is now faded in with sound effects of electronics, motors, sonar devices and other effects appropriate to an ultramodern submarine.

Everbody is now inside the submarine, and all three sound tracks are contributing to the atmosphere. Then a strange thing happens. The music stops (track 2). The voice of the stranger begins to sound as though it were speaking in a sonic hall of mirrors, with every word trailing off in an infinite number of fading fragments. The couple become frightened, and they ask him what he is doing. Their voices are normal, but getting weaker.

Since the stranger's voice and the couple's voices are being handled very differently, they must be on separate tracks. Track 1 has been carrying all the dialogue, but is now carrying only the dialogue of the couple. Track 2, which had been carrying music, is now carrying the dialogue of the stranger. The voice on this track is being fed through a tape delay echo device which produces the strange effect described (more about this later). Track 3 is still carrying the various sound effects of the submarine running.

The stranger begins to laugh hysterically. He is talking at them almost constantly, deriding their gradual loss of speech. (Their voices, on track 1, are being faded out very gradually.) In the midst of another burst of laughter, the scene cuts to an outside view of the beach, and we see that the whale has disappeared from the beach and is heading out to sea. Music of doom accompanies this long shot, on track 3, which is no longer required to carry the sound effects of the submarine's interior. The music and picture fade out together, and the mix of this sequence is completed.

The mix described above is a very complicated one, even though it uses only three tracks. It was designed to illustrate a wide variety of the effects possible in mixing. The main modes of thought involved in its design were the following: Using the minimum number of tracks that will do the job is very desirable. By freely using available time space on any of the tracks, for any material, two or three extra tracks can often be avoided. There is no need to regard a dialogue track as reserved for dialogue only, as long as there is significant blank space in it that can be used for something else.

Whenever two sounds are to be combined, or whenever two parts of the same sound are to be handled differently, they must be run on separate tracks. The relative proportions of each sound can thus also be controlled and changed at will, and each of the parts of a sound may be run through different filtering or enhancement circuits.

If manipulations of the mixing controls are to be made after one sound on a track and before the next, then sufficient space must be allowed for the mix operator to have time to make the changes. Otherwise, the sound juncture must be separated by putting the sounds on different tracks. For example, if some music is to be faded out very quickly at the end of a shot, and a voice speaks immediately at the beginning of the next, the mixer will be required to fade the music all the way out, and then try to get the volume control fully open again in time for the voice. A fraction-of-a-second error here would clip off the first word and require doing that whole section over again.

Sometimes the addition of an extra track can be avoided by using what is called a tape loop. This means that a sound, such as surf, is recorded on 1/4-inch tape and a section about three feet long is spliced to its own beginning, forming a loop. When this is put on a tape-playback unit, it will produce the sound of surf indefinitely. The fact that it is the same waves over and over again will usually not be noticeable. In the mix about the whale, this technique would have made most of track 2 available for other sounds, if it had been necessary.

It is possible to make mixes without the use of a studio and its equipment if the tracks are not required to be in strict synchronization most of the time. For example, if the mix about the whale had not required any sync dialogue, it could have been done with 1/4-inch tape recorders. The parts that needed verbal explanation could have been written as offscreen narration rather than as dialogue. The equipment required to do your own mix would be four good tape recorders, a very inexpensive transistorized volume-control mixer with at least three channels, and connecting cables to hook all this hardware together. The three separate sound tracks would be prepared on separate rolls of recording tape. The surf and the foghorn would be placed on two of the recorders (these could also be just playback decks, since they need not be capable of recording), and the voice narration on the third. The fourth tape recorder would be threaded up with a roll of new tape, and would record the combined outputs of the other three. In terms of the *design* of the sound, almost the same thing is being accomplished in the tape mix as was in the interlock mag film mix. By sacrificing strict sync, which the tape system is not capable of, we are able to use equipment costing only a tiny fraction of the equipment in the studio.

Since we are now dealing with four tape recorders and one projector, getting them all started together can be a bit tricky.

You are going to need at least one helper. In the leader at the front (head) end of the picture film, punch a hole two feet (80 frames) from the first frame of picture. Thread the projector so that this hole will be projected within a few seconds after starting. On the head end of each of the three tracks make a mark 25 inches ahead of the point on the tape that corresponds to the first frame of picture. Thread up the three tracks so that their marks are right at the playback head.

The mix is begun by turning on the recording tape machine, in the record mode. Then turn on the projector, quickly putting your two hands on the start controls of two of the tape playback machines. Your helper will start the third one. At the

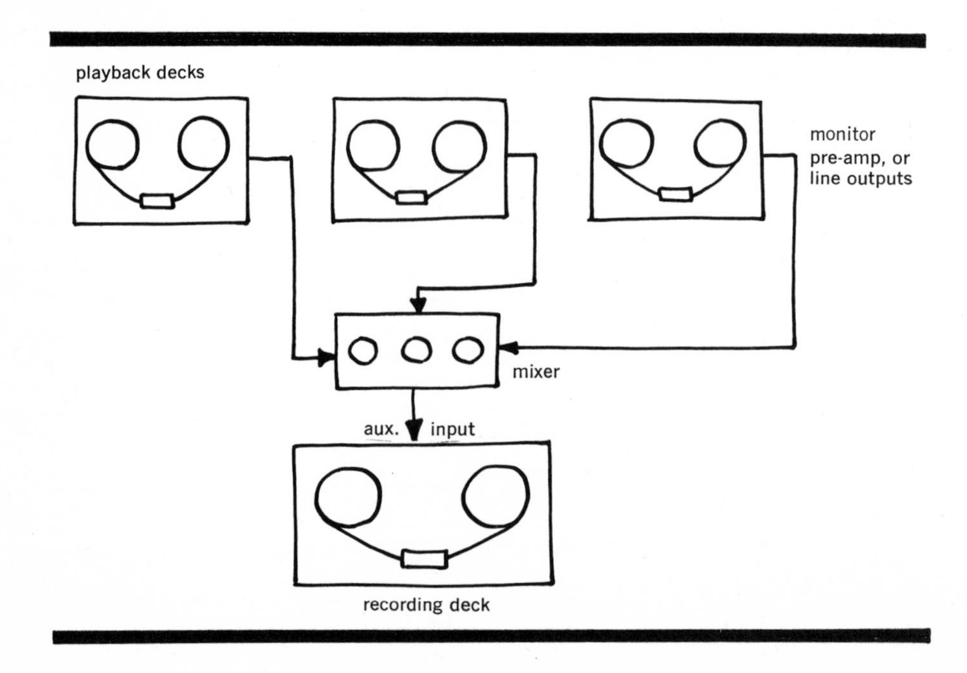

instant that you see the punched hole flash on the screen, turn on all three playbacks together. You now have 3.3 seconds to sit down and get your hands on the volume controls of the mixer box before picture and sounds begin.

Here are some helpful hints. Practice making the mix several times before you actually record one. Mixes require very tricky coordination and fast thinking at times, and learning to keep a cool head comes only with practice. With masking tape, make a label next to each volume control on the mixer, indicating the main sounds on that particular track. In the heat of the mix, it is hard to remember what sound is next on what track. When you are editing the sound tracks, it is best if you can edit each track on the same machine it will be played back on, so that the fact that different tape machines run at slightly different speeds will not affect your track timings. You can use a stereo playback deck to take the place of two playback machines, by re-recording one of your tracks onto the alternate stereo channel of one of the existing tracks. When this is played back, one track will play out the left channel and the other out the right channel. You can also reduce the number of separate tracks by premixing tracks before the main mix. If you had four tracks, and only had machines enough for mixing two, you could mix two of them together, then mix the other two together, leaving you two composite tracks to be mixed. However, the quality of the sound deteriorates a little with each copying of a copy, so it is best to use this technique only with sound effects, and to try to keep the dialogue and music tracks as virgin as possible.

If a complete mixed-sound track contains a significant number of spoken words that must be understood, it is best that other sounds be sacrificed during the spoken passages. The psychological effect of sound effects and music is approximately the same at moderate sound levels as it is at loud levels (dancing to music excepted). But the psychological value of words that must be understood in order to enjoy the film is present only when they are loud and clear enough in relation to other sounds to be intelligible. In other words, language in a film needs much more pampering than do the other sounds.

The mixing session is the first time a film is presented with all its component parts together. The days of dreaming, planning, preparing, shooting, recording and editing have finally brought the film to life, and the baby's first cry is heard in the mixing session.

20

preparing for composite prints

From the creative standpoint your film is completed. You have an edited work print and a mixed sound track to match, and the only thing that is left is to have a composite print made at the lab, in which the picture and sound are printed onto a single strip of film, and in which any dissolves and multiple exposures to be made by the lab are included. The first time that the lab tries to make a composite print of your film is always a little chancy because of the large number of opportunities for a mistake, either by you or them. For this reason this first print is usually called a "first trial answer print." This chapter is concerned with preparing the picture and sound materials for first trial answer printing, and is written in the hope that all your first trial answer prints may be the last of the trials.

The magnetic sound track will first have to be transferred to what is called an optical sound track. The purpose of making an optical sound track from your mixed magnetic track is to put the sound into a visible or photographic form, so that it can be easily printed along with the picture portion of the film. The accompanying photographs show an optical sound track all by itself, and then the same track combined with the picture in a composite print ready for showing. When you take your magnetic sound track to a lab in order to get an optical track made from it, you will need to know some minor but very crucial things about just what kind of optical track you want. First, the emulsion position of the optical track must match the emulsion position of the original picture material; otherwise, they simply cannot be printed together into a composite print. If you shot on a 16mm reversal film, then it is almost certain that your emulsion position is the one called "B" wind. This can be verified by looking into the camera and seeing if the pulldown claw is on the right-hand side of the film (see photo). Thus, if your composite prints are going to be made from the camera original, you will need a "B" wind optical track to match the picture material.

The other main thing you need to know is whether you need a negative or positive track. This also depends on the type of film stock used as camera original. If you will be printing from black-and-white negative, then you will need a negative optical track. If you are printing from black-and-white reversal, then you will need a positive track. If you are printing from color negative, then you will need a negative track developed for color printing. If you are printing from color reversal stock, then it would seem logical to get a positive track, but here the film manufacturers provide a surprise. The standard color-printing films have a special strip of negative emulsion along the edge where the sound track is printed, and so a *negative* optical track is used when making composite color prints from reversal color camera original. To summarize the designations of optical sound tracks, it need only be remembered that the emulsion positions of the picture ma-

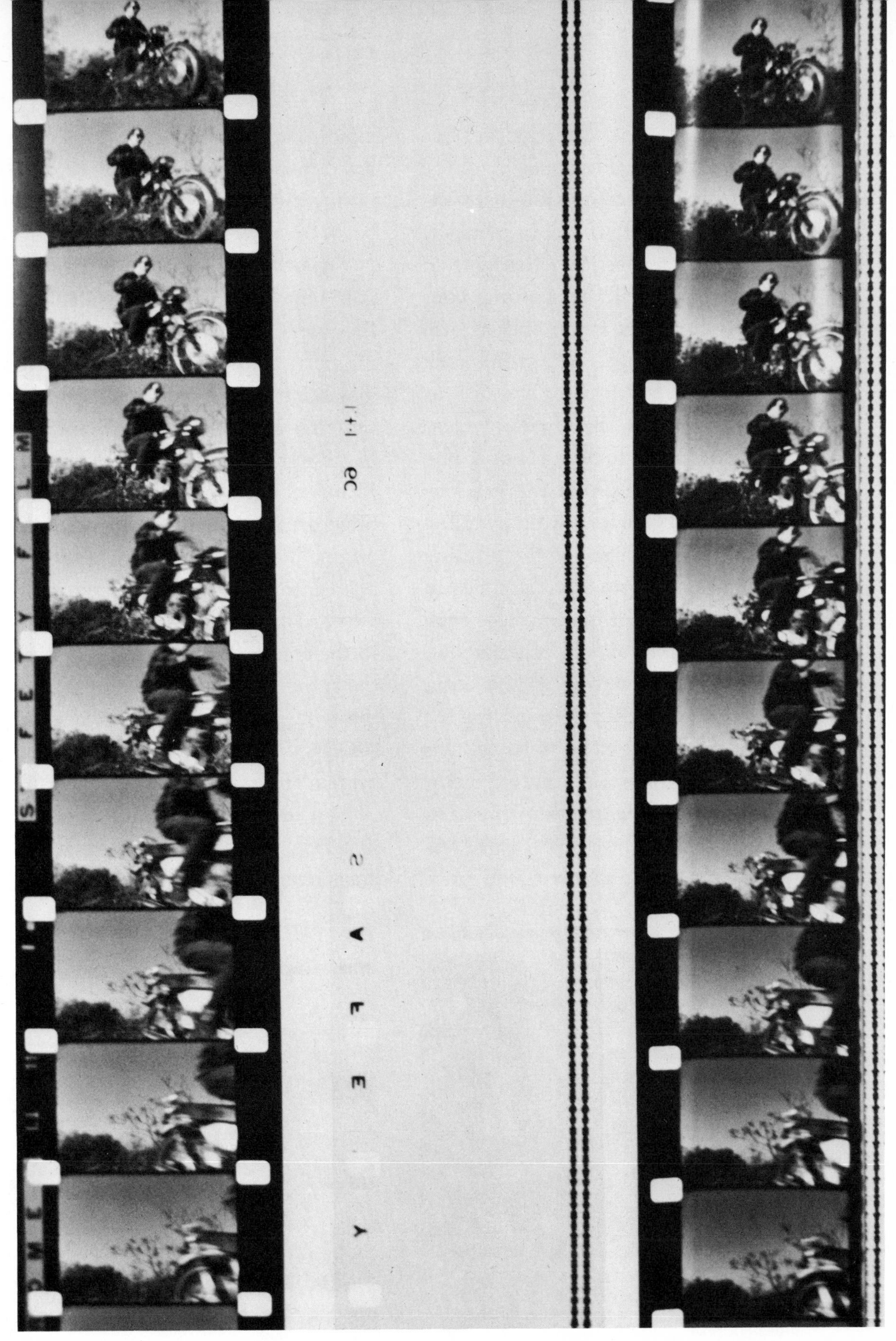

The original footage and an optical sound track are printed together to produce a composite print.

terial and the sound tracks must be the same, and that the *polarity* of the optical must be compatible with the picture material. If doubt persists, tell the lab technician what type of material you will be making your composite prints from, and he will tell you what type of optical track you need.

In cases where hundreds of composite prints are to be made of a film, it is all too likely that the precious original will be damaged in handling or by being worn out on the printing machines. It is standard practice to have some sort of intermediate copy made from the camera original, and then make composite prints from that. This affords protection for the irreplaceable original, and sometimes allows for economical printing methods, reducing the cost per print. The optical tracks, however, are still made according to the same principles discussed above, so that they are compatible with whatever material the picture is going to be *printed* from.

The next thing you will need to do is to match each of the cut scenes in the work print with the corresponding portion of that scene in the original camera footage—which all this time has been (hopefully) kept safe in a film can. After putting on white cotton editor's gloves so that your fingerprints will not damage the original, put the first shot of the work print into the sychronizer and roll it forward a few inches until you come to the edge number printed between the sprocket holes (see picture). Lock the synchronizer with this number straight up, then roll through yoûr original footage on the rewinds until you find this same number. The numbers progress by one digit, increasing as you go toward the end of

The transport claw of this camera engages the sprocket holes on the right side of the film, and thus composite prints made directly from this camera original would require a B wind optical sound track.

Work print and the original camera footage lined up by their edge numbers (represented for illustration by the little pieces of tape marked 5).

the roll. How often the numbers occur depends on the camera stock used. In 16mm it is quite common for them to be spaced at six-inch intervals. Thus if you are looking for a shot numbered 1620 and the beginning of the roll is numbered 1420, you will know you can find the shot you are looking for 100 feet further on in the roll. When you find the edge number you are looking for, put the shot into the synchronizer with the edge number in side-by-side alignment with the number on the work print. Unlock the synchronizer and roll the film toward the head end of the shot. When the first frame of the work print is lined up with the right-hand edge of the synchronizer (see picture), cut the original footage through the middle of the next frame to the right. This extra half-frame is to allow for making the cement splice later, in which process it will be cut off. Then roll the film through the synchronizer in the other direction, toward the tail end of the shot. Cut off the original footage a half-frame to the *left* of the end of the shot in the work print. You now have a piece of cut original footage that corresponds exactly to the first scene of the work print. Using this procedure you just keep matching up the shots in the work print with the corresponding shots of the original until you have compiled a roll of cut original scenes (taped together so you can roll them up) that conforms to the work print.

All this is a very simple operation and usually presents no difficulties more serious than boredom.

If your film contains multiple exposures, dissolves, fades in and out, which are to be created by laboratory printing, it is always a good idea to first mark the work print with stand-

The original is being snipped off a half frame ahead of the scene in the work print it is being matched to (represented by white leader).

The tail end of the original is snipped off a half frame after the end of the corresponding scene in the work print.

ard symbols for fades in and out, for multiple exposures and for dissolves (see diagrams). This can be done with a yellow grease pencil on the emulsion (dull) side of the work print. Not only does this help you keep track of what you are doing, but when given to the lab, along with the other materials for making a composite print, will help them do a good job.

Maybe you want a title superimposed over your first scene. In this case, after matching the background scene with the corresponding shot in the original, make the first frame of the workprint background scene even with the right-hand edge of the synchronizer, as before. The title shot (this must also be camera original) is then laid in the synchronizer side by side with the background. Roll the material forward for as long as you want the title to be superimposed, and then lay in black leader from that point on until you come to the end of the background scene. For the time being, roll this up with all the rest of your cut original. The procedure just used applies to any sort of superimposure you wish to have printed in.

Now, suppose you have a shot in the work print that you wish to have dissolve into the next over a period of two seconds. Notice that the symbol for this effect indicates the superimposition of a fade in of the second scene onto a fade out of the first scene. This means that you must cut the original of these two scenes so that the tail end of the first scene extends past the splice in the work print, and continues until the end of the fade-out marking on the work print. Then the head end of the second scene must extend by an equal distance ahead of the splice in the

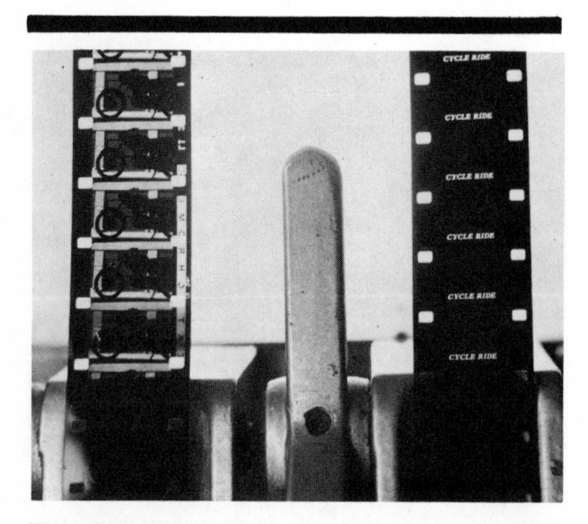

The white title letters on the B roll will be printed on top of the motorcycle on the A roll.

work print (see picture). To do this, you first match up the head ends of the shot in both the work print and the original. You then roll forward to where, in the work print, the first shot is spliced to the second one. (One of the advantages in making dissolves in the camera is that you get to see them in the work print, and you do not have to set them up as we are about to do.) The splice in the work print represents the *middle* of the dissolve, where the two scenes will appear simultaneously on the screen at equal brightnesses. Since the splice marks the middle of a two-second dissolve, you roll the original of the first scene 24 frames (one second) *past* the work-print splice and cut the original through the middle of the 25th frame. This means that this scene will last one second past the middle of the two-second dissolve—just what is desired. Now, line up the original and the work print of the scene to be dissolved into, and roll toward the front end of the shot in the work print, until you get to the same splice as before, which marks the middle of the dissolve. Roll *ahead* of that splice 24 frames and cut through the middle of the 25th. By cutting the original of the two scenes to be dissolved together in this manner, you have provided a total of 48 frames of overlap, with which the lab can make the two-second dissolve.

As soon as all the original shots and titles are cut to length and rolled up in the same sequence as they appear in the work print, the next step is to arrange them so that superimposures will be automatically printed in the right places, and at the same time so that the splices (in 16mm) will be made invisible in the composite prints. The pattern of the arrangement that will accomplish both these aims is called a checkerboard assembly. Here is how it is set up. The very first scene of the film is placed in the synchronizer. In the adjacent gang, the opaque black leader with the title shot is placed in side-by-side sync. This material is rolled through the synchronizer onto *separate* reels. When you get to the tail end of these two strips of film they will be in side-by-side sync, since that is the way you cut them before. Now, with the ends of the film at the top of the synchronizer wheel, and the wheel locked, open the rollers on the gang that contains the background shot. Hold the end of this shot in place on the sprocket teeth, take the end of a roll of black leader and place the sprocket holes at the very end of this onto the sprocket teeth coming through the last frame of picture (see picture). Gently close the rollers to hold this all in place and put a little piece of ¼-inch masking tape over the two strips to hold them in place. Then, open the other gang, which has the end of the black leader in it, and take the second shot of the film and attach it to the end of the black leader in the same manner as described for the background shot. The pattern of what you are doing now is to put each successive shot of the film onto alternate rolls. One of these rolls we will call *A*, and the other *B*, so as to avoid confusion. The first shot of the film goes into roll *A*, and at the same time, we put a piece of black leader into roll *B*, which is exactly the same length. When you get to the end of the shot in roll *A*, you put the second shot of the film onto the *B* roll and, at the same time, an equivalent length of black leader onto the *A* roll. The

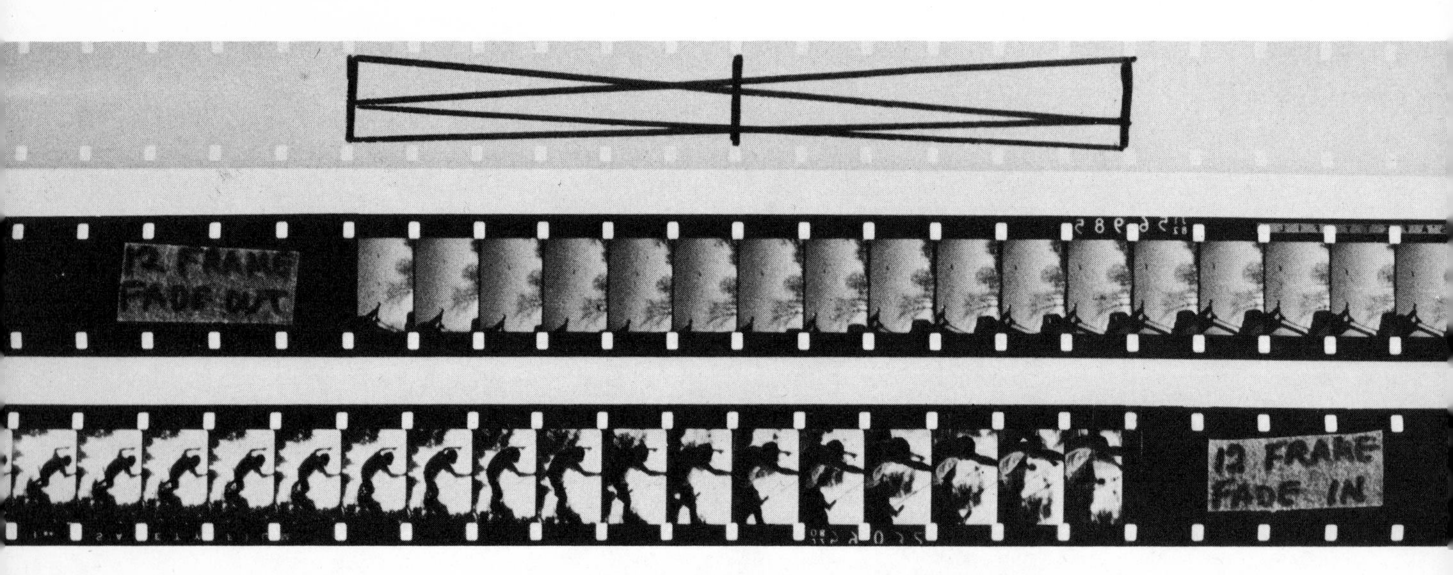

A 12-frame dissolve set up in an A and B assembly. The fade in (made in the laboratory printing machine) will be superimposed upon the fade out, as indicated by the markings on the work print (represented by the white leader).

third shot goes on the *A* roll, the fourth on the *B* roll, and so on until the end. That is all there is to checkerboard assembly, which has confused, confounded and exasperated many newcomers to film. The picture of a section of checkerboard assembly makes it clear where the name came from, and what the geometrical configuration is. The exceptions to the pattern occur when you want material to be superimposed.

The next thing to do is to make printing leaders. The printing machines at the lab have lots of rollers and sprocket wheels in them and require several feet of leader for threading. Also, the leaders provide identification of the film material, and they indicate exactly where the start marks are for picture rolls and sound.

To make them, take three seven-foot lengths of white leader and write the information on their emulsion side as shown. Then put the front (head) ends of all three in the synchronizer side by side. Roll them through the synchronizer until you are about two feet from the ends. Make a sync mark on the *A* roll and the *B* roll of picture, side by side, and mark them "printer sync." Then turn the movable-frame counting plate on the front wheel of the synchronizer so that "0" frame is directly under the sync marks you have just made. Roll the leaders on through the machine to the right a few more inches until the frame number "26" comes up. On the frame of the optical sound leader, make a sync mark directly above the 26, and label this "printer sync." The sync starting marks you have made should thus be side by side for the *picture* rolls, but the start mark for the optical track should be 26 frames to the left

After opening the rollers on one of the gangs, put the sprocket holes of the next piece of either black leader or picture onto the sprocket teeth which project through the last sprocket holes of the material already on the wheel.

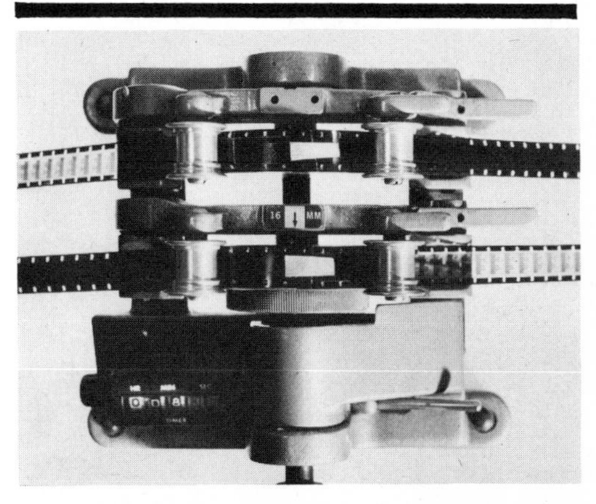

The picture material and black leader in the right-hand side of the synchronizer end together at the center of the picture. The next scene of picture is then taped to the end of the leader, and black leader is taped to the end of the first scene.

of these. The reason for this oddity lies in the design of the projectors. In the picture, notice that the frame of film that is being projected is a few inches behind the frame of sound-track area that is being scanned. This distance is 26 frames. On the composite print the picture and sound have to be printed 26 frames out of step because the projector picks them up out of step. By following the start-mark procedure discussed, the correct displacement of sound and picture will be printed automatically by the lab.

Now, roll the leaders through the synchonizer until you come to the tail ends, and cut them all off evenly and *exactly*. These ends of the leader are now in *editorial* sync, that is, side by side. Once you have established the *printer* sync marks on the body of the leaders, forget about them, because you will now be setting the material in sync by aligning it side by side. Splice a piece of black leader two feet (80 frames) long onto the end of the *A* roll and also the *B* roll. This completes the preparation of the leaders for the head end. The formats for head- and tail-end leaders shown are typical, and they will work even though there are variations from lab to lab.

At the head end of the optical sound track there will be a frame of very regular wiggles, which is the visual representation of the beep tone recorded from the head end of the magnetic track. Splice the optical track onto the leader for the sound track in such a way that the visible beep is the very first frame of the optical that occurs (see picture). Since you had placed the beep on the magnetic track exactly 80 frames (two feet) ahead of the first sound, the optical track will now automat-

A checkerboard printing assembly (consisting of shots only a few frames long, for illustration).

In the projector, the optical sound track is scanned by a light beam as it passes over the roller at the lower right of the picture. Since this position is 26 frames ahead of the frame of picture being projected through the lens, the sound track must be printed 26 frames ahead of its corresponding picture.

ically be printed in correct relationship to the picture rolls, since two feet of black leader (80 frames) precedes each of them. This is not quite an orthodox way of putting leader to the optical sound track, but it has a couple of advantages over the usual way. It is simpler and more direct, and in the case of negative tracks, it minimizes the amount of track noise heard just before the film starts.

The leaders for the *A* and *B* picture rolls can be taped into place, with their emulsion position the same as that of the original, and when this is done all that remains is to splice all this material together. A type of splicer known as a hot splicer must be used at this point. You can rent one for two or three dollars for a day, which is probably all the time you will need it. This splicer is designed so that all of the overlapping of two pieces of film spliced together occurs on the *right*-hand frame only (see picture). This leaves the frame of picture to the left of the splice entirely unmarred by the splice. This factor, combined with the checkerboard assembly, is the secret of how splices can be made invisible in 16mm composite prints. Remember that each of the picture scenes in a checkerboard assembly is preceded and followed by opaque black leader. If you put the black leader on the right-hand side of the splicer, and the picture in the left, then the overlap (or disfiguring) area of the splice occurs entirely on the black leader, not at all on the picture. Since the leader is opaque, the fact that there is a splice there will not print onto the final print. In order for the method to work, it is clearly necessary that all splices be made with the black leader in the right-hand

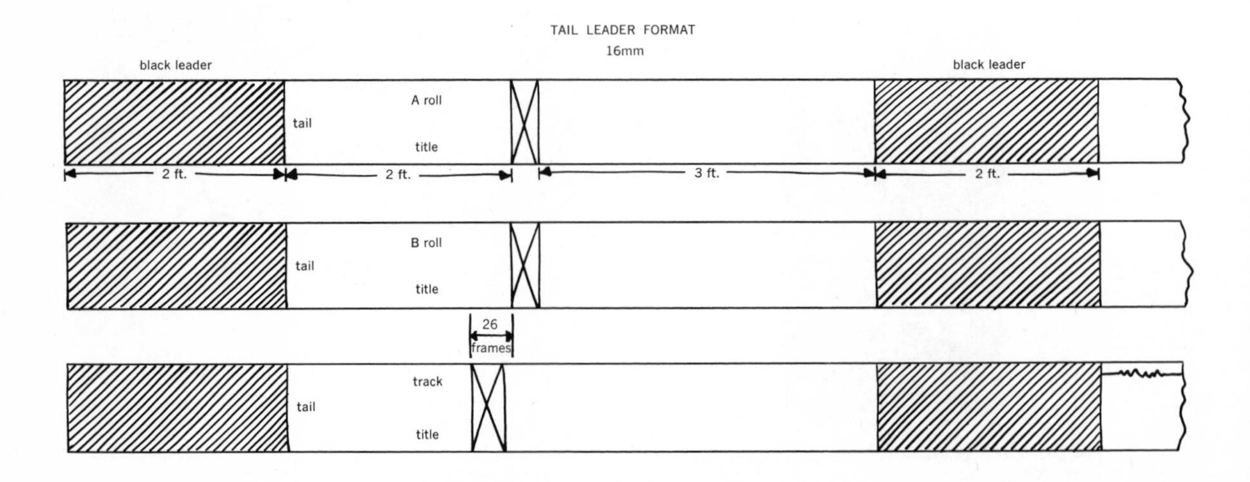

side of the splicer. The easiest way to do this is to make *only* those splices in which the leader is on the right, as you go splicing through the roll. When you get to the end, take the reel of film and put it back on the left-hand rewind; now, since the reel is turned around, all the intended splices that you skipped the first time through will be turned around with the black leader on the right, and you can complete the splicing.

When everything is spliced, including the leaders, it is a good idea to thread everything up together and run the picture rolls and sound through the synchronizer for one last careful check to see that everything is in alignment. Try to find any mistakes now, before they show up in a wasted first-trial answer print. In order to correct mistakes, you can always add or cut out sections of the black leader in the checkerboard pattern, thus changing the alignment without cutting up picture material.

When you are satisfied that things are set up correctly, roll up each of the rolls, emulsion side out, onto a plastic core, using a split reel (see picture). Put the rolls and the marked work print in a film can labeled with what is inside and to whom it belongs. You are now ready, either with sublime confidence or with trepidation, to take your film to the lab for printing.

Here is how the checkerboarded *A* and *B* rolls work in the lab: They print the *A* roll onto a roll of printing film that has no sprocket holes down one side (so that the sound track may be printed there). Wherever there is a scene of picture on the *A* roll, it is, of course, exposed onto the print film. But where there is black leader, the printing light can-

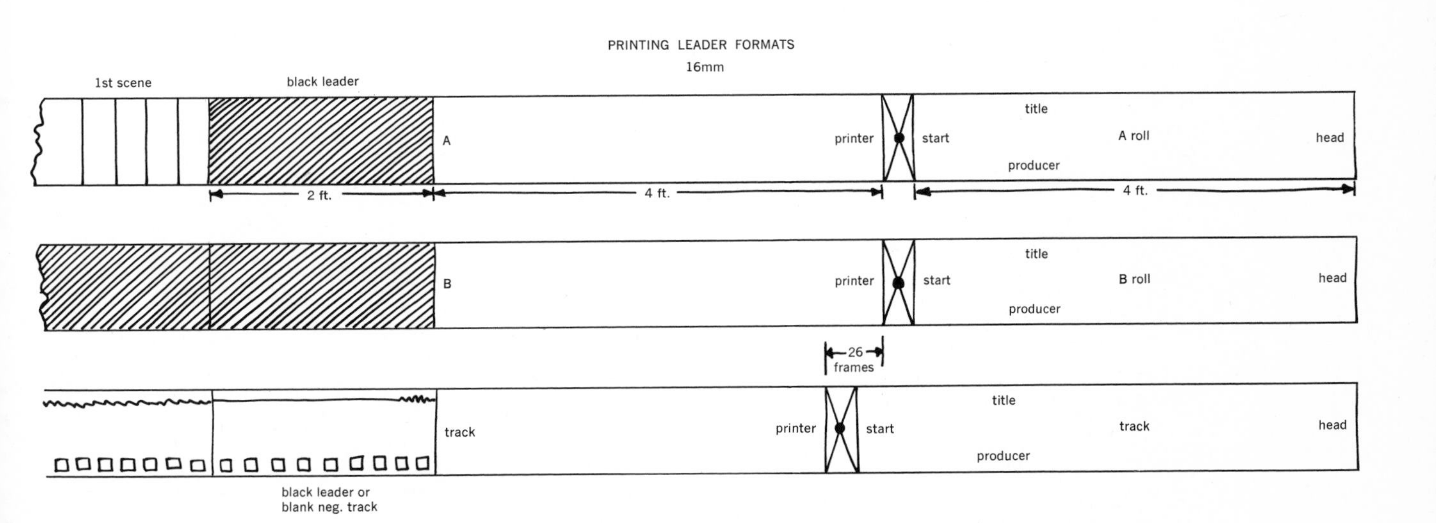

not shine through to the print film, and that section of film remains blank. Then, the print-film roll is wound back to the beginning, and another run is made, this time shining the printing light through the *B* roll. Since the picture scenes in the *B* roll correspond exactly to the blank spaces left after the *A* roll was printed, this printing run fills in all the blank spaces. Printing roll *B* does not disturb what was already printed with the *A* roll, because the opaque black leader sections in roll *B* block the printing light from reaching the previously exposed *A* roll sections. Where superimpositions are to occur, there is picture material on *both* rolls simultaneously. Remember, we set up the background scene (the first shot of the film) on the *A* roll, and put the title shot side by side with it on the *B* roll, which will cause the title automatically to be printed on top of the background shot. In the case of a dissolve from one scene to the next, the first shot of the dissolve will be on one roll, and the shot which is dissolved into will be on the other roll. Since we assembled that junction so that the second shot begins 48 frames before the first one ends, there will be a two-second superimposure. To make this imposure come out as a dissolve, the lab makes a two-second fade-out of the printing light at the end of the first scene of the dissolve, and then, when they are printing from the other roll, they make a two-second fade-in on the scene being dissolved into.

In addition to this, a lab man called a timer will look at each shot of your original and evaluate it in terms of what printing light exposure will make it look best. This tends to even out exposure varia-

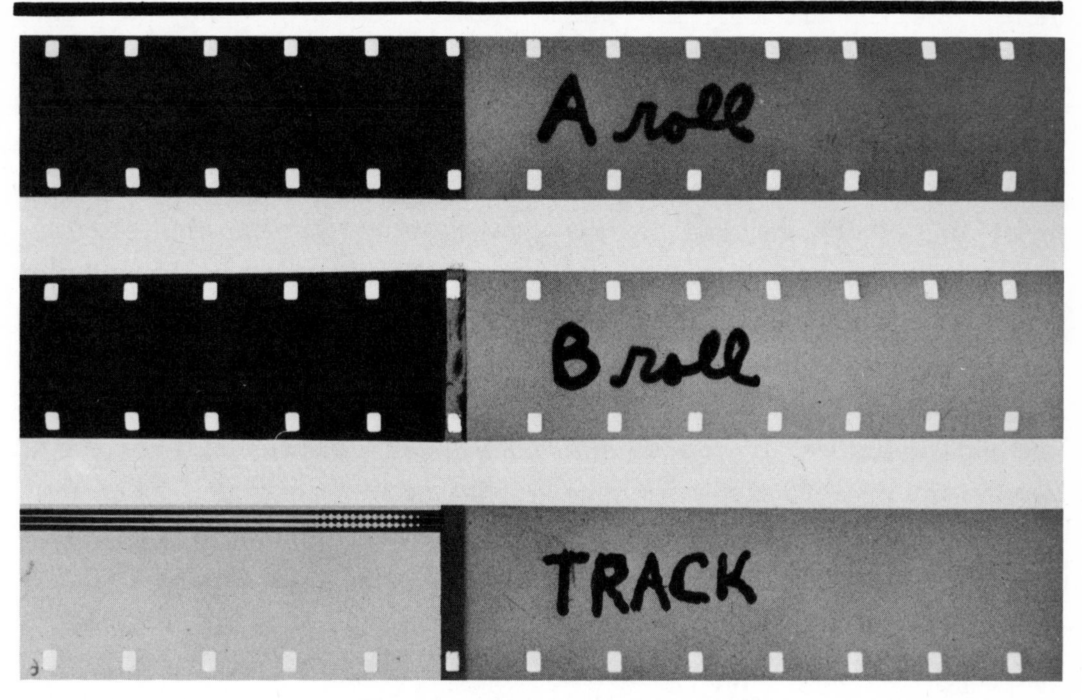

Two picture rolls and their sound track in editorial (side-by-side) sync. The beep tone is visible as diamond-shaped modulations on the track.

A splice made with a hot splicer throws all the overlap area onto the adjacent black leader where it will not print onto the composite print.

tions in the original photography and provide a better tonal flow. Small degrees of color correction may even be introduced at this stage. This process is called timing, and is almost universally included in the instructions for the first trial answer print.

As always, there are shortcuts that may be taken instead of the complete methods described. If you do not require any multiple exposures to be made by the lab, and you are willing to bypass the invisible splices, then you can skip making the *A* and *B* rolls, and splice all your shots together in a single roll. If you are also willing to put up with some loss of photographic fidelity in terms of definition, contrast, color, and graininess, then you need not make a work print from your original and would therefore not have to do any scene matching (conforming) of original to work print. The most direct thing you could do would be to shoot film, edit that same material (the original) and have that printed together with an optical track (using the leader format described), and thus come up with a composite print. The result of the full-dress method is substantially superior, so when making a film for a sponsor you should simply include it in the budget. But there are many occasions when the shortcut methods will do the job desired, and it is good to keep them in mind as alternatives.

The two flanges of a split reel may be separated and put back together again. This allows film wound on plastic cores to be handled very quickly without a lot of reels and rewinding.

21

filmic expression

Film-making is not a craft of the abstract. It is very dependent upon one's experiences in life, and one's conclusions about those experiences. When he is working at his best, the film-maker makes a film to express his involvement with some facet of his life which at the time is preeminently fascinating to him. Notable examples of theatrical films imbued with immense personal involvement include *Joan of Arc, Triumph of the Will, Citizen Kane, Four Hundred Blows, La Dolce Vita, Morgan, Chappaqua,* and *Woman in the Dunes.*

In all of these, the fascination to the film-maker was so intense that it resulted in the use of somewhat new filmic forms of expression. A film, on the screen, is only moving shadows. Its sound track is only pressure ripples in the air. But by intelligent and inspired design of these forms and ripples, an audience is moved. Without the appropriate and effective design of the forms, the content is never brought to life. We see this often in the works of beginning artists in all fields; little hints of passion and communication, but without the forming of the medium in a way that has meaning and power.

We need to try some hypothetical pieces of filmic design (design meaning the arrangement of component parts into a form for a purpose). We can postulate a theme, a feeling or a point of view, and then try to develop a filmic form to express it.

Suppose you see the comfortable middle-class life as represented on television—in the form of product ads and soap operas and discussion programs—in ironic contrast to the concerns of the people of a tenement neighborhood. What we desire is to make this contrast, this lack of connection, poignantly clear. One of the formal ways in which this could be accomplished would be to have the picture portion of the film do the representing of one of the two worlds, and the sound track represent the other. The two worlds correspond with each other scarcely at all, and so the sound track will not correspond with the picture. The very fact of the clash between the two elements of the film produces a strain in the audience's mind, which is trying to make the picture and sound go together. This turns out to be very nearly impossible, which produces just the effect intended. The fact that the representations of the two different cultures will not harmonize with each other becomes an *experiential* matter, personally felt by each member of the audience. This is much more powerful than would be some form that merely *told* the audience about the difference. A shot looking down on the street from high overhead shows lots of people milling around, not going anywhere in particular. The sound track, taken from the introduction to a Western series, says, "Americans turned their faces to the West. They poured into the new territories by the thousands. . . ." At this point we see a shot of a little wagon being pulled along with empty wine bottles in it, "Bringing their household possessions . . ." Now a shot of a pile of debris, "Climbing the mountains . . ." Now a shot of a large puddle in an empty lot, several boys trying to make a part of a discarded refrigerator serve as a boat, "Crossing the mighty rivers . . ." Next perhaps, shots of the crooked rooftops and crumbling chimneys, shot in stark contrast, like a broken desert landscape: "It was a hard land, a hostile land . . ." A shot of a delapidated tenement—the camera tilts slowly up toward a pair of patched windows, "And so Cinderella left her sisters . . ." In the windows can now be seen reflected the gigantic white structure of a luxury high-rise apartment building, "And went to live in the palace, where she lived happily ever after."

This filmic structure works because of the way in which it teases the mind. It talks about people doing things, and you see people doing things, so you think that the two should be in harmony. It instantly becomes apparent, however, that there are sharp discrepancies between what the track says and what you see—and it is this *difference* that is the most important and the expressive part.

The use of sound to modify the effect of the audience's reaction to the picture is universal. A frequent device is to put some light, up-tempo, modern jazz, over scenes of violence in a television series. This has the effect of soothing the audience into thinking it is just sort of a game, and not anything to be alarmed about. It allows the audience to have its cake without qualms. But let's carry this principle further. In a sequence that takes place in the rain, a young girl cannot get her umbrella to stay open. A young man happens by, likes the look of her, saunters over to help with the tricky umbrella, and a sequence follows in which he finally gets it to stay up. At the point in this sequence when it is apparent that she is also attracted to him, it is the sound track which reacts to this happy awareness, with a tune and lyrics about sunshine, how it is shining down and warms a fellow's feet as they touch the ground, and that it's a good day because of all the sunshine. In the picture they are both dripping wet, the whole scene is in gloomy gray, the rain is pouring down. The contrast between picture and sound is understood by the audience as the contrast between physical situation and emotional situation. In this case it is the camera which is seeing what they are doing and where they are, and it is the sound track which is expressing for the characters how they are feeling. This use of sound is quite distinct from the carefree jazz laid over violence in that it is an expression of the feelings of characters in the film.

Now let us try designing a picture sequence that is expressive of an emotional (interior) situation. A girl who has been getting increasingly anxious about the pressures and tensions of big-city life has begun to long for some sunshine and quiet in the country. She looks out of an apartment window, sees the huge buildings towering up over her, and begins to feel trapped. Just then, from a clock tower, a bell tolls. She thinks of this as a funeral bell, and that she is being buried alive in the city.

This sequence could be done several ways. Her own voice, offscreen, could say lines that verbally express her upsetting vision of her situation. This will work, but it is essentially a literary rather than a filmic solution. She could shriek and rant and rave, and then tell a friend who rushes in what she had just experienced, but this is mainly a theatrical solution rather than a filmic one.

A more interesting way to present this sequence would be to design a flow of images and sounds related to the real elements of the situation as already described, which will directly affect the feelings of the audience, as though they were able to experience her feelings for a while.

We can start with looming buildings. Framing the shot so that the tops of the buildings are at first near the bottom of the frame, we can slowly tilt the camera downward, causing the feeling that we are sinking down into their depths. At the same time we can fade in a re-recording of the bell being played back at half speed over the original realistic one. The octave-lower tone will gradually dominate, and the duration of the tolls will stretch to twice their length. We could also change the color at this point, by using a deep-blue filter that would render the scenes in monochromatic blue and black. Now the buildings are closing in from all directions, this being accomplished by multiple exposures made with the same slow tilting action as the first one. By shooting with the camera on its side and upside down, and moving the framing slowly in the appropriate direction during the takes, we can get images of the buildings closing in from all directions. Then we could bring in images of doors closing, the girl starting to come out toward the camera; now the doors swing ponderously shut, and she is lost from view. This too, could be shot through a blue filter, and a large variety of bizarre angles of the door's motion could be shot with a wide-angle lens. The shots should be framed to make the doors look as massive and as unstoppable as possible. We could make many such shots, some with the door edges swinging past the lens, others with the camera moving with the door itself, so that it is the door frames that seem to move on the screen. The disorientation thus produced serves the purpose of removing the familiarity of everyday doors, and gives the total impression only of relentless closing. These shots can be cut very short and very repetitively so that the motion of closing, of being blocked out of view, becomes a relentless wave that cannot be escaped.

The sound track during all this could be provided with very slow labored breathing, as though a person were in danger of suffocating. Along with this, and the tolling bells, we could use menacing deep organ tones at intervals, or the crashing of the lower strings of a piano, made by pulling on them directly and suddenly letting them go.

With all these elements working together, the film expression of the girl's feelings becomes very powerful and direct. This power is the result of combining a number of techniques into a design for a specific communication of feeling.

In the feature film *Morgan,* there is a very effective use of brief cutaways to various animals as an expression of the hero's state of mind. When he suddenly feels free and light, he moves in an imitation flying motion that match-cuts directly to a large bird swooping in flight, and than cuts back to the hero in a match cut that continues his imitation flying motion. When he is frustrated he starts to pound his chest like a gorilla, and this cuts for a moment to a gorilla doing just that. These cutaways are used throughout the film, and as the audience becomes familiar with the format, this cutting arrangement becomes an integral fiber of the weave of the film. It works because the quick cutaways are very brief and do not interrupt the flow, because they are very cleverly cut according to the principles of matching the continuity of motion, and because they are a consistent element throughout the film, relating meaningfully to the mind of the hero.

To conclude this chapter it would be interesting to design an entire short entertainment film. For a story line, we can begin with the old fairy tale, "Little Red Riding Hood." The original version told of a very young girl (virgin), who had to go through the woods to her grandmother's cottage in order to bring her a basket of goodies. She is warned to be careful of the wolves, (males) but on her way she meets one anyway, who finds out where she is going and takes a shortcut to get there first. When Little Red arrives at the cottage, it is not Granny who is in the bed, (a suitable place for lovemaking) but the wolf in disguise. Then follows the famous dialogue that concludes with Little Red saying, "Why, Grandmother, what a big mouth you have!" — to which the wolf replies, "All the better to eat you with, my dear!" Which he starts to do, but a woodsman hears the commotion, rushes in with his ax and saves the girl.

Most psychologists who have looked closely at this story agree that it is a parable designed to impress young girls with the knowledge that their own newly developed sexual attractiveness is a danger to them and that they must be careful. This was a very serious matter to the culture that produced this story, but to the people reading this book, the story is downright funny. Once we recognize this, we can deliberately push the inherent humor further in the design of the film version, thus anticipating where the audience is going to go emotionally, and being ready for them with a good show. Here it is as it might appear on the screen, with the salient technical manipulations mentioned as we go along, and with the camera angles and editing structure and some of the sound all described when they are of special importance.

Fade in as Little Red Riding Hood, who is a very attractive young girl, straightens her little red miniskirt, brushes her long red hair out of her eyes, picks up a little basket of cookies, and hails a horse-drawn open carriage. (This should all be done at a leisurely pace, since it is an introduction to a lyrical part of the story.)

She climbs up into the carriage and starts to sit down (cut). Since the fact that she is a very attractive female is paramount to the story, this shot should be frankly arranged to emphasize this.

She completes the motion of sitting down (match action from previous cut) and arranges herself neatly and primly. The driver (who is in the foreground of this wide-angle shot) cracks his whip.

The horse pulls on his yoke and they all start off down the road.

It is a lovely warm Spring day. We establish this through the following sequence:

Medium closeup of Little Red, her head back-lit by the sun, which shines through her long hair, falling loosely over her shoulders.

Dissolve to trucking shot past a field of colorful wild flowers.

Dissolve to horse's hoofs clopping merrily along.

Dissolve to full screen shot of spoked carriage wheel turning (camera trucking along beside wheel).

Superimpose medium closeups of Little Red back-lit by sun flaring into lens. She tilts her head back, enjoying the warmth, and shakes her hair. (Determine exposure by measuring her face close up.)

(Fade out the superimpose of her, but retain the wheel.)

Dissolve from wheel into long shot which looks through a lot of trees and sees the carriage pull up to the edge of the woods and stop. (These dissolves could be made in the camera. If this cannot be done, then the shots can be made separately and dissolved in the lab by means of the *A* and *B* roll assembly. See Chapter 20.)

Looking down from up high in the trees, the camera sees Little Red get out of the carriage and venture into the woods. She is seen here as a tiny figure, now quite alone, in the woods. (This shot would need to be hand-held, using a wide-angle lens.)

A wide-angle shot of Little Red in medium-close shot. She is looking up and around at the woods, showing some apprehension. (Appropriate music will make this twice as effective.)

The camera is looking through a forest of dark treetrunks (by using a telephoto, more trees can be gotten between the camera and Little Red) and sees her walking through the woods in the distance. (Mix in scattered sounds of wild animals hooting and howling eerily.)

A wide-angle shot of the girl walking toward the camera. (Some follow focus will be necessary.) As she comes into full facial closeup, she suddenly freezes, eyes big with fright.

Cut to medium closeup of animal fur (we are too close to it to see just what sort of animal), then camera tilts slowly up to reveal a young man in a very shaggy fur coat, leaning casually against a tree.

Big closeup of her staring at him.

Cut to a close-up of his face. He looks somewhat like a wolf, because of two very long upper canine teeth, which his lips do not cover (false, of course) and very shaggy hair, wicked-looking long black eyebrows and mustache, and unusually large dark eyes (makeup) which glow with flickering yellow light (reflections of a small spotlight with a yellow filter, or superimpose something appropriate at the *A* and *B* stage).

He smiles and says, "My, what a pretty young woman you are! Where are you going with that basket of goodies?" (This picture and sound should be shot with synchronous equipment operated from batteries. If not, it could be dubbed in later with interlocked equipment.)

She looks as though she is in a trance, but manages to answer, "I'm on my way to Grandma's cottage, to bring her these homemade cookies."

He is still smiling slightly, and looking at her appreciatively. He doesn't say anything.

Closeup of her, feeling that she should say something. "I'm sure she will like them."

Wolf is rubbing his chin contemplatively. "And where does your Granny live, my dear?"

Camera is now looking over Wolf's shoulder at Little Red, who says, "By the meadow, in the orange cottage."

In a medium closeup, Wolf rolls his eyes: "That's very interesting, my dear. Perhaps I . . .

Cut back to over-the-shoulder shot of Little Red, who interrupts Wolf to say, "Now, if you will excuse me, I must hurry on to Grandma's." She starts to move out of frame. Camera moves out from behind Wolf as he turns his head to watch her go, camera ending up in medium closeup of his face as he says, "Hmmmm . . . by the edge of the meadow." (Their conversation is shot in separate pieces of closeup for maximum editing flexibility.)

In a very long shot, with the camera fairly high up, Wolf can be seen zigging and zagging at breakneck speed through the woods (camera running at 8 frames per second, or less).

Wolf comes to a log that serves as a bridge across a stream, and he zips along its length on one foot, as though skating. (Single frame animation. Camera will have to be on a tripod.)

He zips to a pile of leaves and easily leaps up a ten-foot ledge. (Reverse motion of him jumping down backwards into the leaves.)

In a long shot with the orange cabin in the foreground, Wolf can be seen scooting around the place, looking in the windows and then dashing in the door.

Little Red is skipping along through the woods, somewhat in a hurry now.

Wolf is in the cabin, wiping his greasy mouth on his sleeve; then he picks a little piece of chipped bone out of his teeth.

He runs to the window, looks out, and sees Little Red coming into view.

He jumps into bed and puts on Granny's little bonnet.

Outside the cabin door, Little Red walks into frame and knocks on the door. (In the previous five alternations of shot from Wolf to Little Red there has been considerable compression of time to keep the action developing briskly and to avoid showing Wolf gobbling up Grandma.)

Wolf is seen in medium closeup, frantically trying to disguise himself as much as possible by means of the bonnet, the bedcovers, and a little pair of metal-framed Granny glasses.

Closeup of Little Red looking concerned, as she knocks again.

A male voice says, "Who is it?" Realizing the mistake, the voice rises in pitch to a falsetto as it says again, "Who is it?"

Wide-angle shot with Wolf sitting in bed in foreground; door of cabin opens in background, and Little Red bounces in exclaiming, "It's me, Granny (she comes up close), and I've brought you a basket of goodies."

Medium closeup of Wolf nodding enthusiastically.

Medium closeup of Little Red looking at Granny quizzically. "Why Grandma, what big . . . (cut to Wolf's eyes) "eyes you have!"

Wolf, seen in medium shot, says in his sweetest falsetto, "All the better to see you with, my dear."

Little Red is seen standing in full-length shot, looking very good indeed. At rapid intervals there flash extremely brief cuts of Little Red in various states of provocative undress. (We are presenting Wolf's imagination at work, by means of insert shots only 6 frames in length.)

"Why, Grandma . . . (she leans over for a closer look) what big ears you have!"

A closeup of the ears as they turn red. (An extremely wide-angle lens used in conjunction with a camera motion bringing the ears into frame as foreground objects will effect an apparent enlargement. The reddening could be done with a filtered spotlight.)

Medium shot of Little Red leaning over him, toward camera. (She is lit very glamorously and shot through considerable lens diffusion.) She is saying, "I've never noticed before . . . (her voice fades out as she continues talking, and cross-fading in is a romantic tinkle of thousands of tiny angel bells and sweet singing voices; this will be done in the mix.) Her voice cross-fades back in, saying, "How do you keep them warm in the Winter? My, they certainly are large."

Closeup of Wolf returning to reality as he hurriedly says, "All the better to hear you with, my dear."

She sits down on the edge of the bed, facing him.

Under the sheets we can see his hands slowly lifting up, getting ready to grab her.

Closeup of Wolf, licking his lips. "Grandma!" cries Little Red. He immediately tries to look like Granny again. She continues, "What a big mouth you have!" (This paragraph would be shot as a single take for Wolf, and the same for Red. Notice that when it is edited it will be cut into four shots.)

The camera is at bed level, looking straight up at the ceiling, Wolf is included in the framing. He speaks, starting out in his Granny voice, "All the better . . ." He rises slowly up out from under the covers, looming up as a giant figure over the camera (the wide angle emphasizes his height).

Little Red's expression changes to stunned alarm as she tilts her head upward, staring at Wolf (this would be an excellent place for a zoom in).

Cut back to Wolf rising. "All the better to eat you up, my dear," he thunders in his true voice. (Wolf revealing his true identity has been expanded in time by the cutaway to Red's reaction, and the continuation of Wolf's rising shot without taking any time out of it to compensate for the addition of the cutaway. This is a dramatic moment and it is best to maximize it.)

(In slow motion) Little Red flings herself backward on the bed in an effort to get away.

(Slow motion) Wolf flings himself toward her in a swan dive.

(Slow motion) She pulls up her knees.

(Slow motion) Wolf lands belly first on her braced knees, knocking the wind out of himself (sound of air being let out of a balloon). (Since to actually stage the above would probably damage Wolf beyond repair, the action must be broken up into key component pieces for photography, and the event made to take place cinematically by clever editing.) Wolf falls on the floor beside the bed.

Little Red (still in slow motion) makes a dreamlike float toward the door. Just as she gets there, Wolf somehow instantly appears standing in her way (stop action, with camera on a tripod). She turns and slow-motions toward the window. Wolf instantly appears there too.

Medium shot of Little Red. In desperation she covers her eyes.

She is instantly standing all by herself in a field of black.

(Her image size and position must match in these last 2 shots).

Closeup (very) of her fingers uncovering her eyes. There is Wolf again, right in front of her, looking dashing and confident.

As a last resort she runs for the bed (normal motion) and hides under the covers. Wolf then scampers over to the bed, but on the way . . .

Closeup of Wolf stubbing his toe against a chair leg. (This should be staged a little more slowly than real time, because the screen speed in large closeup is increased.)

Long shot of Wolf hopping over to the bed, holding his foot with one hand and yelping.

Medium closeup of Little Red peeping out from under the sheets to see what has happened.

Long shot of Wolf lying on his back on the bed, holding his foot in the air and sounding very much like a coyote (a sound effects record will help).

Medium shot as Little Red takes pity on him and strokes his fur to ease his pain.

Wolf strokes her hair tenderly in return appreciation.

She smiles very slightly and begins to look more closely at Wolf.

Wolf, in closeup, doesn't look so fearsome after all, as his fangs slowly disappear, then his extra hair and weird eyes, and finally his face is transformed into that of a rather good-looking young man. (This effect requires three takes, each with the camera and Wolf's face in exactly the same frame positions. The first take of him completely wolfy, is dissolved into the second take with some of the makeup removed, this is dissolved into the last take, where he is totally human. This transformation sequence might be intercut with reactions of Little Red.)

A closeup of the look on Little Red's face reveals that she finds him attractive and that she is pleased about it. (This might require some ingenious elicitation on the part of the director.)

In medium shot, Wolf kisses her forehead, then her lips. They roll into each other's arms.

The camera is outside the window looking in. Into the edge of the frame, outside the window, creeps a form.

Looking toward the window, from the inside of the cabin, we see a commando fully equipped with automatic rifle and purple beret. Zoom into closeup of his face peering through the window at the lovers. It is distorted both by the snarl of dislike on his lips and by the wavy window glass through which he is seen.

From his side of the glass, we see what he thinks he sees. A shaggy wolf molesting a poor innocent maiden.

The commando crashes through the window, levels his automatic straight at the camera lens, and blasts away.

Red sits up bolt upright in terror, Wolf is next to her, represented only by a crumpled fur coat.

"What have you done?" she screams. "You've killed him, you've murdered him, you madman!"

The commando looks confused. "I was only following orders, Ma'am. We've been told to secure this whole sector from the wolf menace."

Red shakes her head in dismay. She sobs, "Oh, I wish you had never come here. (Echo, echo, echo . . .)

We seem to be flying through celestial clouds as we hear reverberating echoes of Little Red's heartfelt wish. (The clouds could be made from smoke from burning rags, back-lit against a dark background, or they could be shot on negative black-and-white and be of India ink poured into water. The reverberating echoes are made by feeding a delayed playback of an original recording of her words back into the recording circuit.)

Dissolve into a complex control panel as a satin-robed arm reaches into frame and flicks a switch.

Cut to the smoke and fire from the commando's weapon going back into the muzzle. The commando leaps backward through the shattered window, which reassembles itself, and the commando is gone.

Little Red, in medium shot, ecstatic with joy.

Long shot of the bed on which the young man is unfolding himself from a crumpled position (sans fur coat).

"Oh, Wolfie," says Little Red, "you're all right again!"

"Little Red," says Wolfie, "you've made a miracle happen."

Closeup of her face, her brow knit a bit.

"Wolfie?"

He looks at her expectantly.

"Where do you suppose Granny is?"

THE END

In making this hypothetical film we have needed to use techniques and design principles from nearly every chapter in this book. If you were actually to make this film you would find yourself, at every step in its design, running through everything you could think about creative manipulation of the film medium, to see what could be used to make the film rich in visual and sonic elements, deft and dramatic in pacing, and *expressive* of the story.

In order to give an idea of how the costs for producing this film could be estimated, the following budget is presented. It contains the basic costs that are common to most types of films (see following page).

Instead of spending this much money, serious sacrifices could be made to come within an absolutely minimum budget. If you could manage to shoot at a 2-to-1 ratio, bor-

A Budget for *Little Red Riding Hood*

(assume) ten-minute running time
sync sound shooting
16mm color
3-to-1 ratio of shooting footage to screen footage
A and *B* roll checkerboard assembly
all services and equipment to be paid for

type 7255 original stock (1100 feet)	$ 80.00
processing the above	55.00
work print of above	100.00
camera rental for 1 day (Eclair npr for sound)	40.00
recorder rental for 1 day (Nagra)	35.00
camera rental for 2 days (Bolex Reflex)	30.00
rental of cabin (3 days)	75.00
lighting units for cabin interiors (6 units, 3 days)	30.00
quartz bulbs for lighting units	45.00
actors for 3 days (2 leads at $35 per day)	210.00
props, costumes, makeup, transportation, etc.	100.00
printed credit and title cards	20.00
transfer of ¼-inch tapes to magnetic film	50.00
mag stock for above (1200 feet)	30.00
black leader for checkerboard	20.00
rental of cutting room with required equipment (4 days)	120.00
interlock mix (1 hour)	60.00
optical sound track	40.00
first trial answer print	70.00
	$1,210.00

row all the equipment and the props, use entirely volunteer labor, if you do not make work prints or set up *A* and *B* printing rolls, use dubbed-in or offscreen voices instead of sync, and are willing to put up with visible splices and mediocre print quality, the budget could be . . .

800 feet Kodachrome II (with developing)	$ 88.00
optical track (neg.)	40.00
first trial answer	70.00
	$198.00

By commercial-industry standards, the larger figure would still be considered a very low budget, sometimes called a "shoestring" budget.

These two budgets represent the range of costs involved in the making of *Little Red Riding Hood.* Since the difference between the two budgets represents costs which it is possible to reduce by means of ingenuity, persuasion, good fortune, and sacrifice of some quality, it is possible that the actual cost of production could be anywhere between $200 and $1,200.

Now that we have reached the end of this book, it is hoped that the basic principles of professional film-making have been presented in a way that interests you.

Film is a young and growing medium, and its uses and its powers are constantly being expanded by people who combine a talent for the medium with a vision that they want to share with the world. May this book be a help toward the expression of that vision.